Coffee Sh

MW01289320

COFFEE SHOP
CONVERSATIONS

PSYCHOLOGY
AND THE
BIBLE
LIVE, LOVE, AND LEAD WELL

Jed Jurchenko

Coffee Shop
CONVERSATIONS
BUILDING LEADERS, GROWING RELATIONSHIPS

www.CoffeeShopConversations.com

Praise for
Coffee Shop Conversations

"Jed has a passion for helping people sharpen their leadership and relationship skills at home, work and everywhere they go. *Coffee Shop Conversations,* which reflects Jed's love for God and for people, is a tool to help you make your life count!"
~ Pastor Jim Garlow, *Senior Pastor: Skyline Wesleyan Church*

"*Coffee Shop Conversations* makes learning psychology and theology easy and engaging. The practical principles taught in this book are quickly learned, and easily applied. I would highly recommend this book to students, parents, spouses, and any looking to grow in their leadership and relationship skills."
~ Al Menconi, *Al Menconi Ministries*

"Jed's *Coffee Shop Conversations* delivers biblical answers to real-life issues. It will enrich your Christian life — well worth your investment. I encourage you to read it while opening up your life to God's GRACE."
~ Dr. Donald W. Welch, *Ph.D., LMFT, Founder and President, Center for Enriching Relationships*

"It is encouraging to have a guide like Jed use his knowledge and life experience to usher us through the clinical frame in order to get to the biblical heart of where joy and peace can reside!"
~ Doug Swink, *Winning at Home Ministries*

"Jed does a wonderful job with this book... If you grew up in the church, you will probably relate with some of it and you will be blessed by the rest of it."
~ Adam Smith *AGBeat Top 50 Influencer 2014*

"If suffering has put you on the sidelines, then the healing insights offered by Mr. Jurchenko will certainly give you both the tools and encouragement you need to get back on track."
~ Dr. J.R. Miller, *Author: More Than Cake: 52 Mediations to Feed your Team*

"Using principles of Psychology that affirm Biblical truths, Jed shares his own Journey of pushing through adversity to living a Christ-filled life. Jed shares not only his knowledge, but the wisdom that comes with having emptied himself before a loving God. So pour a fresh cup of coffee. Definitely worth the read!"
~ Chris Rader Author: *Unconditional Dad: A Father and Pastor's Journey Through the Words 'Dad, I'm Gay.'*

"An insightful and tender exchange where biblical truths and psychological principles intersect. Enjoy this refreshing and poignant resource that goes beyond "good advice" while authentically revealing the golden nuggets that can truly penetrate a broken heart."
~ Ramona M. Garretson, *Psy.D., MFT, NCC*

"In a practical way Jed illuminates how psychological principles are the workable servants of ultimate truth, the Bible. He treads with discernment the narrow path of using enough of personal experience to identify with real folks without bogging down in a slough of subjectivity. Simply put, the teaching is helpful, the read is enjoyable and thought provoking, it lands in the right place...God's truth."

~ Pastor Lindell Quam, *Senior Pastor: Elim Lutheran Church*

A casual, coffee shop style conversation
providing practical tools from the Bible and psychology
for living, loving and leading well.

Printed by CreateSpace,
An Amazon.com Company
Available from Amazon.com
and other online stores

Dedication

To my incredible wife Jenny: Thank you for your love and encouragement, and for partnering with me in this adventure of living out life's greatest lessons. Our adventure together is better than I could ever have imagined!

To Mackenzie, Brooklyn and Addison: Your compassion for others shines through daily. Your actions demonstrate that children are never too young to live out the lessons found in this book. We are truly blessed to have such wonderful daughters.

Contents

*****

Foreword

I have heard it said that "if you always do what you have always done, you'll always get what you have always gotten". In other words, if you find yourself in a hole, then stop digging. When people are in a crisis or in a panic mode, it is almost impossible for them to think their way toward a solution. The brain is constructed in such a way that it (anger, fear, and depression) turns the "solution" part of the brain off and then searches the immediate short term memory for a quick rudimentary solution. Once it finds something that seems to have worked in the past, that's what it chooses. In other words, when we are panicking or depressed, we can't always think our way out of a problem.

A client once told me that she thought I was a genius because I could think of all kinds of solutions for her problems. I told her I'm not a genius; I'm just not depressed (or panicking). We have better access to the solution part of our brains when we're calm.

One way to get someone to access the solution part of their brain is to get them doing something. This sends a signal that calms the emergency response system and allows a person to better access the solution part of the brain. Three things begin to happen: we minimize our "stinking thinking," we become better aware that we are dropping "Anger-nades" on others, and we lower our stress levels.

It has also been said that a person with experience can out debate a person with just knowledge any day of the week. Jed does a wonderful job employing his personal reflections and proven life experience to help the reader to integrate biblical and proven psychological principles to tackle life's seemingly debilitating problems. The Bible is the greatest psychology book ever written. I was struck by Jed's respect for others as he gently leads the reader along a journey that he himself has gone before.

Dr. Barry Lord
~ *Professor Emirates Southern California Seminary*

Introduction

Psychology, the Bible, and Coffee

Q: How Does Jesus make his coffee?
A: Hebrews it!

Welcome to *Coffee Shop Conversations on the Bible and Psychology*. This book is for all who desire to create positive changes in their life and in the lives of others.

As you may have guessed by now, I love coffee. Whether it's the international franchise across the street, or one of the many eclectic, hole-in-the-wall coffee shops throughout San Diego County, there is something amazing about a good cup of coffee and the entire coffee shop experience.

In these lively, highly caffeinated environments, friendships are strengthened and creative ideas are born. Coffee shops are where people gather to do life together: struggles are shared, challenges are overcome, and victories are celebrated. It's the ideal background for the principles taught in this book—principles that lead to closer relationships, decreased conflict, stronger leadership, and greater overall well-being.

This book contains key principles taught by therapists, pastors, and life-coaches for increasing positive outcomes by learning to live, love, and lead well. Living well involves taking care of ourselves so that we can enjoy our God given time on earth to its fullest and give to others out of a place of abundance. Loving well means caring for others in a way that is helpful—as opposed to having good intentions that produce poor results, and leading well entails meeting those around us where they are at, then gently guiding them to a healthier and happier way of living. The lessons found in this book are time-tested and have been applied by a multitude of people throughout the centuries. When put into practice, these principles work.

It may come as a surprise to discover that the majority of these lessons were written in the Bible long before they developed into the foundational principles of psychology. Although the Bible and psychology have been portrayed as being at odds with one another in the past, this book is different because it demonstrates how psychology and the Bible work together to produce dynamic life change. This book is pro-Bible, pro-psychology, and pro-you.

Another thing that I love about coffee shops is that they are places of honest conversations. The come-as-you-are atmosphere sets the tone for keeping things real. Walk into a coffee shop early enough and you may find people sipping on their favorite beverage while wearing their slippers, pajamas, or robes. There is no facade here — this is as real as it gets. Keeping things real, simple, and practical is another goal of this book. In the forthcoming chapters, we will dive into some deep concepts from theology and psychology, yet every conversation will ultimately be steered back to making these principles work.

In the pages ahead, we will examine key concepts from six of the primary counseling theories. Each chapter begins with an introduction to the theory's formation, and every chapter is packed with Scripture in order to demonstrate how these ideas fit into a biblical worldview.

While understanding how each theory works is a good start, it's imperative to move beyond a mere intellectual understanding to putting these principles into practice. Throughout the book, you will find a multitude of tools for taking action. Key ideas are summed up in italics, and questions that promote deeper growth are included at the end of each chapter.

As a marriage and family therapist, pastor and college professor, I have seen first-hand the variety of ways positive growth takes place. Sometimes it occurs after gaining deeper insights, while at other times it happens as a result of being reminded of simple truths we already know well. My hope is that this book will provide you with new insights into human behaviors as well as inspire you to further develop the key principles you are already familiar with.

While *Coffee Shop Conversation on the Bible and Psychology* is for everyone desiring to create positive life change, I am writing specifically for three groups of people. First, this book is for those who are hurting and find themselves in the midst of life's storms. Chapter 1 begins with the story of my own personal crisis — a crisis that led me first to the church, then to psychology, and ultimately to the Bible in a search for healing. I know what it is like to experience crisis first hand.

After reading hundreds of books in the areas of theology and psychology, graduating with Master of Divinity, going back to school to complete a second master's degree in counseling, and becoming a licensed marriage and family therapist, I have discovered that there are no secrets to avoiding life's challenges. The bad news is that, while we live, difficult times will always lurk in the future. The good news is that there is an abundance of wisdom that can help us move through these challenges with dignity and grace. At times life is hard, but by utilizing the principles in this book, we can make sure that life is not any more difficult than it needs to be.

On the other hand, there are also stretches where life is fun, funny, and filled with wonder. The second group for whom this book is written is for those experiencing the joyful periods in life. It is for everyone who desires to continue growing by building on their current strengths.

If you find yourself in this stage of life, I believe that you will be pleasantly surprised to find a multitude of tools for making the most of these satisfying times.

I'm fortunate enough to be in one of those places right now. I am married to a wonderful woman, have two beautiful daughters, and the four of us are excitedly awaiting the arrival of a baby girl. In the midst of life's pleasant moments, the principles in this book help us to enjoy and build on the successes we have.

Finally, this book is for everyone who longs to understand how psychology and the Bible work together hand-in-hand to produce dynamic life-change. This book was, in part, the result of ongoing discussions with the students I teach at Southern California Seminary. It has been a great joy to watch these students' faces light up as they apply key teaching from psychology and the Scripture to their own lives and experience first-hand the positive changes that result.

Whether you are currently trudging through life's storms, seeking ways to further your own growth, or wanting to better understand how principles from psychology and the Bible team-up to create vibrant life change, this book is for you. Although life is difficult at times, it's possible to move though these challenges gracefully, and during the moments when life is beautiful, fun, and funny, applying the lessons in this book allows us to enjoy these pleasant moments to their fullest.

Whatever stage you are in right now, it's my hope that these lessons will add value to your life so that you thrive in the journey ahead. So grab a cup of coffee, tea, or another favorite beverage, and let's get started!

Sincerely,

COFFEE SHOP CONVERSATIONS

One

Discovering Life's Greatest Lessons

Guidance for life's calms and storms

In storms of life, you need to sit back,
relax till the storm is gone and be able to
pick yourself up and live again.

~ Author Unknown

The goal is to move through challenges gracefully and to enjoy life's amazing moments to their fullest.

Have you ever taken one step forward, only to take two, three, or even five steps back? If so, then you and I have a lot in common. If you've ever fallen down and struggled to get back up again, you will have a good understanding of how I felt in September 2005.

This book begins with a story about a time I fell... hard. Fortunately, I had some good friends to help me back up. I'm excited to introduce you to many of them in this book. Some I have the privilege of knowing personally, while others, I'm only familiar with through their writings. However, all of these men and women have added value to my life. I have learned much from them and I am excited to pass on this information to you. But before I introduce them to you, I would like to first share the story of how I first encountered the principles taught in this book. Whether you are currently hurting, growing, or thriving, I think that you will be able to relate to many of the experiences I had during my journey of discovery.

Falling

I was 28 years old when my path took a sudden twist toward the unexpected. Life's storms came crashing down, leaving me feeling confused, broken, and overwhelmed. In less than a year, my once calm, smooth world had flipped upside down. If my childhood had not been so sheltered, perhaps these events would have felt somewhat less traumatic. However, this was not the case, and these unexpected events led me down a path far different from the quiet life I had become accustomed to.

I was born in July of 1978 to two devoted Christian parents. From birth, I had literally grown up in the church. My dad served as the junior-high ministries director in a large church near our family's home, and my birth meant an instant addition to the youth group. I'm told that I spent so much time there that my first steps occurred in the sanctuary. As you can imagine, faith had an important role in my life from the very beginning. Growing up, we had family prayers, family dinners, and family devotionals. Our family attended church functions multiple times a week and, as I grew older, I became an active member in the church youth group. After completing high school, I attended college and eventually transferred to a local seminary where I graduated with a

Masters of Divinity, a seven-year Bible degree, which I completed in exactly seven years. While attending Seminary, I began serving in the same church my dad had worked at the year I was born. I started as an intern and in time was hired as part of the pastoral staff. Of course, life wasn't perfect. There had been occasional bumps in the road, but even those had been few, far between and were quickly forgotten.

Crisis

A crisis is defined as a time in a person's life when their stress level exceeds their capacity to cope. In 2005, I experienced this firsthand as an onslaught of pressures rapidly compiled and surpassed my abilities to manage them successfully. Feeling lost, hurt, and confused, I embarked on a journey searching for answers to the challenges I faced. Along the way I would discover the many valuable lessons taught in this book. Lessons that would, in due course, result in a life much better than I had imagined. But first there would be years of pain and maturing in the stretches ahead.

Having grown up in the church, it was only natural to begin with the church in my search for answers. With hopeful expectation, I embarked on my journey of meeting with pastors and church leadership in a search for counsel and wise advice. However, much to my dismay, I discovered that many in the church were as confounded as I was... sometimes even more so. It's not that these leaders didn't want to help; I truly believe they did, and many were exceedingly generous with their time. Although these men and women were sincere, in their zeal they would push for solutions that were sincerely wrong, encouraging actions that did more harm than good.

For the sake of privacy, I won't go into the specific details of the crises I was facing, but will instead give a more general description. If you are going through some of the same struggles, I want you to know there is hope. There are answers out there as well as many people who are equipped to provide caring support and wise advice. However, it may take some searching to find them.

During my time of crisis, I was looking for ways to support loved ones and family members struggling with issues of mental illness, domestic violence, a recent suicide attempt, a close family member who was arrested, and one who was making repeated threats to have an abortion. In addition, I also found myself facing a personal financial crisis and the possibility of a divorce in the works. And to make matters worse, this all hit at once, during a period when I was going through a major career change and a move out of state.

It's difficult to describe the flood of emotions I experienced during this time. Anger, frustration, sorrow, feelings of emptiness and loss were all there. Some days I wondered if the pain would ever go away. As you can imagine, with all of this going on, I was also in need of strategies for managing my own level of stress.

Living the Definition of Insanity

While some of the people I met with felt unequipped to provide advice, others pointed me in the direction of the "safe Christian answers." These are the "go-to" answers for just about every problem imaginable and include advice to:

- Pray more…
- Do daily Bible study…
- Attend church regularly…
- Worship more…
- Tithe…
- And keep doing these things over and over again, trusting God for the results.

Many people have received advice like this at some point in their life, and while all of these things are excellent spiritual disciplines, none of them directly related to the challenges I faced. If you have ever received similar guidance in the midst of a calamity, then it's likely that you understand just how frustrating this can be. Following God is good, but it is also not a formula for instantaneously resolving problems. Because I was feeling desperate, I decided to put this advice into practice, and when my problems didn't decrease, I tried harder.

Insanity has been defined as "doing the same thing over and over again while expecting different results," and I soon found myself living out this definition. I was "white-knuckling it," holding on as tight as I could, waiting for something good to happen. I felt miserable, but the advice sounded spiritual, so I continued to hold on with ever-increasing times of prayer, Bible study, giving, and going to church while waiting for God to produce the results.

When the desired results didn't come, I began to mentally beat myself up, thinking that there was something wrong with me.

Perhaps God is angry with me?

Maybe I deserve this calamity?

Perhaps this is God's punishment for something I've done?

In my distorted thinking, I reasoned that if I was taking all the right steps and God didn't provide immediate results, then it must be my fault. Little did I know that God was already in the process of answering my prayers, by gently guiding me to a group of people who lived the lessons found in this book.

Lost and Found

I share these snapshots of my life with you because I want you to know that I have been there myself. I have experienced the fiery times of crises and know all too well the torments of emotional and spiritual distress they bring. In my work as a marriage and family therapist, I am well aware that, at times, life is hard. Painful twists and turns eventually happen to everyone. Most people will know what it is like to descend into the depths of crisis at some point in their life. The good news is that the pain does eventually pass and, for some, a painful event will serve as a catalyst for personal growth, self-discovery, and the starting point for a new, magnificent journey.

My search for answers eventually led me back to studying at the seminary I had graduated from a number of years earlier. Returning was difficult. I felt like a failure and certainly didn't feel spiritual enough for a seminary. A few months earlier I had stopped attending church entirely due to feeling judged. It began with conversations at church becoming shorter and increasingly awkward. It was as if my crisis was violating the unspoken church rules of keeping things cheerful, tranquil, and upbeat. As a person facing difficult times, I was rocking the boat. I felt like the black sheep of God's family, too messy to be touched, and if I was missed when I quietly disappeared, it was without my awareness.

As difficult as it was, I am proud to say that I did eventually walk through those seminary doors and, much to my surprise, I was greeted with an experience that was far better than I had expected. My first encounter was with Dr. Barry Lord, the dean of the psychology program. Our time together was brief and to the point, yet it was also very different from my previous experiences. As I told my story, he listened — I mean, really listened in such a way that it could almost be felt. I didn't get the impression that he was anywhere near being overwhelmed by my challenges, and he was certainly not in a rush to try to solve them all at once. Instead, he simply listened. And as he listened I began to think, *If this man is not in a panic over the challenges I am facing, maybe I don't need to be, either.*

Finding Answers

When I finished sharing my story, the dean stated, "You need a job. Jobs are especially important to men and you'll begin to feel better once you start working." I knew he was right. Dr. Lord walked with me to a job board posted outside of his office. He unpinned a newspaper clipping and highlighted several posts from the non-profit section he knew I would qualify for. "If you're going to get a counseling degree, here are the types of jobs you'll want to look for," he said. I thanked him, and took the school information packet along with the highlighted newspaper clippings, as I headed for the door. However, I didn't make it far before I was gently redirected back to the dean's office and an empty desk nearby. "I've got an extra computer here, why don't you begin working on your resume right now?" he suggested. The dean's words were confident and reassuring. He believed in me during a time when I found it hard to believe in myself. It felt empowering and it was exactly the type of help I had been looking for.

I returned home that day to receive a phone call a few moments after walking through the door. It was the seminary dean. He'd found another job that he thought might be a good fit and wanted to let me know right away. He also gave me clear instructions that I was to let him know the minute I was hired. The extra accountability was motivating. Within a few weeks I had completed my background check and began working at a nearby group home. I had found the support I was looking for. I also had a clear path regarding the direction I would take in my ongoing search for answers.

Discovering Life's Greatest Lessons

I was introduced to life's greatest lessons by spending a few moments in the presence of a man who lived them. About a year later, after the birth of my first daughter, I began my initial classes in psychology. Sitting three rows back, in the furthest corner of the classroom, I positioned myself as far away from the head of the class as possible. Our school had once functioned as a Catholic monastery, but had since been repainted and updated with the latest technology. It was an odd mix of old and new. The room itself provided a perfect metaphor of leaving the past behind and moving forward to new beginnings. This tiny classroom would serve as the primary meeting place for our modest band of psychology students over the next three years.

That first night of class, I listened intently as the professor gave an overview of the different counseling theories that we would be studying over the course of the program. While he lectured, passage after passage of Scripture from my seminary days came to mind, and I became increasingly excited about what we were being taught. *This is exactly what the Bible teaches*, I thought to myself. Yet I also wondered why I had not heard this message before and why it had been so difficult to find a community of believers who were willing to talk openly about the more demanding trials of life.

A Bright Future

It has now been over eight years since I re-entered those seminary doors. I'm a licensed marriage and family therapist and have the honor of being a support system for others who are in crisis. I've also had the privilege of returning to the seminary a third time, this time in the role of professor. Life is good… not perfect by any means, but good. The psychology classes, combined with the teachings I received from the seminary, brought hope and led me down a path toward emotional, relational, and spiritual health.

And that is why I am writing this book, *Coffee Shop Conversations on the Bible and Psychology.* I have personally experienced the power of these foundational life lessons and continue to see their effectiveness on a daily basis. These lessons deal with real-life issues and lead down a path of personal, relational, and spiritual growth. The life lessons you will find in the book are time-tested truths, confirmed by the word of God, that help us know how to live, love, and lead well during both the good times of life and during the storms.

Getting Started

Over the years, a number of books have been written about the Bible and psychology. Some of these books discourage combining the two; others wrestle with the deep theological implications of integration. Yet, few books focus on the similarities and combined strengths of the Scriptures and psychology. Sure, there are a few areas where theologians and psychologists disagree, but some disagreement is normal and healthy because it leads to deeper thinking, fresh insights, and new discoveries. It is not uncommon for theologians and psychologists to have disagreements within their own fields and it would be unreasonable to expect that these two would agree on everything.

However, areas where the Bible and psychology disagree will not be our focus. Instead, it is my sincere hope that while reading this book you experience an excitement similar to what I felt during those initial psychology classes—the exhilaration of discovering practical tools and techniques that work. As you begin applying these tools, my hope is that you, too, will experience the joy, healing, and positive life changes that result from discovering life's greatest lessons.

At times, life is hard; at other times life is fun, funny, and wonderful. The goal of living out these principles is to move through life's challenges gracefully, not allowing these difficulties to become any more complicated than they need to be, and to enjoy life's amazing moments to the fullest. There are many reasons why a book focusing on key principles from the Bible and psychology needs to be written. Let's look at four of my favorites:

1. Psychology and the Bible both recognize human brokenness.

The Bible begins in the book of Genesis with the story of creation. After speaking the heavens and earth into existence, God proclaims that all He has made "is good." Adam, the first living man, along with his wife, Eve, find themselves in a beautiful garden called Eden. God entrusts Adam with the task of naming the animals and of tending to the garden. God and Adam have a close connection that culminates at the end of each day when God Himself meets with Adam, and the two stroll together through the garden.

Yet, this time in paradise doesn't last. Adam and Eve make a conscious decision to disobey God by eating from the one tree in the garden that God commanded them not to eat from. As a result of this single act of disobedience, sin and death enter this once good world. God's creation becomes tainted. However, the death that results is not instantaneous; it occurs in a variety of ways, starting with a spiritual death that creates a barrier between mankind and God. Adam and Eve are banished from the garden. They are no longer permitted to walk with God at the end of each day, nor do they continue speaking with Him directly.

In addition to this spiritual death, the process of natural death is set in motion. I would imagine that it only took Adam and Eve a few moments to discover that things no longer worked the way they used to. Muscles began to ache, necks kinked, and accidents at work resulted in bruises and broken bones. Due to straying from God's perfect plan, women would experience pain during childbirth and it would now take many hours of toil for the ground to produce its fruit. In an instant, life became increasingly difficult and painful.

Our human bodies are complex systems formed from over 60 chemical elements, 78 organs, 200 bones, 600 muscles, and a brain consisting of approximately 86 billion cells. Due to the complexities of our bodies, there are thousands of minute malfunctions that can occur, and because of the disobedience of Adam in a garden, years ago, all of the things that can go wrong sometimes do. Bodily hormones and chemicals in our brains get out of balance; thinking becomes skewed; intrusive and unwanted thoughts wreak havoc in people's minds. Anxieties, depressions, phobias, relational problems, hate, anger, and anguish abound… Everything has changed.

This is not to say that everything that can go wrong always does. Instead, we find ourselves caught up in the conflict of a once good world under a curse of sin and death. The earth is filled with wonder, beauty, and awe reflecting the goodness of its creator, as well as the chaos resulting from mankind's falling outside of a right relationship with God.

The Bible and Mental Illness

At this point, psychology picks up the Genesis story by expounding on this new human condition. This is done in the *Diagnostic and Statical Manual of Mental Disorders* or *DSM* for short. As of 2014, the *DSM* is in its fifth edition and contains the classification and criteria for over 300 different manifestations of mental illness. While the specific psychological disorders contained in the *DSM* are not mentioned by name in the Bible, they are very much in alignment with a biblical world view. The book of Genesis describes how humanity entered into a condition of brokenness, and the *DSM* provides a detailed account of what this brokenness looks like… and it's not pretty.

Because our bodies are intertwined systems wherein each cell impacts the next, even minor physical disparities influence the way we think, feel, behave and relate to those around us. Sometimes, the various disorders are the result of personal acts of sinful behavior but, far more often, the signs and symptoms of the 300 plus things that can go psychologically wrong with mankind are the result of being born into a broken world.

Research shows that the lifetime prevalence rate of contracting a diagnosable *DSM* disorder is 46.4 percent.[1] This means that nearly half of the Americans are affected by mental illness at some point during their lifetime. Those in the other 53.6 percent, the ones who are fortunate enough not to meet the full criteria of a diagnosable disorder, will suffer from many of the signs and symptoms of these disorders in spite of the fact that they do not meet the full criteria. We have all been impacted by the garden events.

2. Psychology and the Bible are in the restoration business.

Although examining the human condition of brokenness isn't fun, it is necessary. We must first recognize that we are wrecked before we can begin the process of restoration. This brings us to a second area where the Bible and psychology are in agreement; both are in the restoration business. One of my favorite verses in the Bible is John 10:10, where Jesus says that He has come so that we can have life and have it more abundantly. And that is exactly what Jesus does: He provides restoration. While alive on earth, Jesus:

- Healed the physically sick (Matthew 4:23).
- Encouraged those living in disobedience to, "go and sin no more" (John 8:11).
- Offered rest to the weary and heavy hearted (Matthew 11:28).
- Gave Himself to restore the broken relationship between God and mankind (John 3:16).
- Rose from the grave defeating death, then ascended into heaven, showing the world that He is Lord over life, death, and everything else (1 Corinthians 15:3-4).
- And, one day Christ will return, completing His work by bringing ultimate healing to this broken world. Eden lost will become Eden restored. Every

tear will be wiped away, wars will end, and even the animals will live at peace with one another (Revelation 21:4).

As Christ followers, we look forward to the day of His return with expectation and hope while continuing to live in the current reality of brokenness. This is where psychology again comes into play. While psychology does not offer complete restoration, it does provide temporary relief from suffering by offering strategies for improving physical and mental health in the here and now.

We might say that, in small ways, counselors and psychologists seek to provide healing like Jesus did. Every person Jesus healed in His earthly ministry eventually fell sick again. The physical healing brought temporary relief, but it was incomplete. When we are sick, we know that regaining our health is good, even if it is only momentary. There has never been a time in my life where I was ill, whether it was with a cold, flu, or chicken-pox, that I have not been elated to get better. In John 14:12, Jesus talked about His followers doing even greater works than Him, and one of the works that God calls believers to do is to provide support to those who are suffering.

One goal of learning life's great lessons is to live well, or to bring healing and relief to ourselves and to others. I state that we bring healing to ourselves first because we cannot impart to others that which we do not possess. In learning and applying life's great lessons, we want to begin with ourselves so that we can reach out to others from a place of health and abundance. It's similar to a flight attendant providing instructions for adults to first put on their own oxygen masks during an emergency and then to help those around them. We start with ourselves so that in due time, we can provide support to others.

3. Psychology and the Bible have a high regard for the truth.

A third area where the Bible and psychology are in agreement is in their high regard for truth. First, let's explore the importance of truth in psychology. Psychology is defined as "the science of the mind or of mental states or processes."[2] Science holds truth in high regard. In its purest form, a scientific experiment starts with a hypothesis, which is sometimes referred to as an "educated guess." It then conducts tests designed to prove or to disprove this hypothesis. These experiments can be conducted in a laboratory or out in the general public. The scientific community will frequently use surveys and random sample groups (randomly picked people from the general population) for the purpose of proving or disproving their theories.

When conducting surveys, the impact that gender, culture, and age can have on the end result is taken into account. Those who adhere to the scientific process understand that sometimes just thinking that you are receiving help can increase hope and cause someone to feel better. This is known as the "placebo effect," and experiments are carefully designed to account for this occurrence by including a control group in the studies. All of these efforts are put forth for the cause of discovering truth. In the field of science, including the science of psychology, uncovering the truth is everything and thousands of hours are invested in pursuit of this goal.

Truth is equally as important to Christ followers. The Bible calls believers to seek out the truth in a manner similar to scientists conducting experiments. In 1 Thessalonians 5:21-22, the Apostle Paul exhorts believers to "Examine all things; hold fast to what is good. Stay away from every form of evil." Paul chastises the Thessalonians, for being too quick to follow whatever teachings came their way, and encourages them to be more like the Bereans, who searched the Scriptures daily to confirm the message they received was true.[3]

Over and over again, the Bible calls its followers to an intelligent faith, a faith that is based on facts and historical events. To be a follower of Christ means to embrace truth. We have no choice in the matter. Christ Himself said, "I am the way, the truth and the life."[4] To be a Christ follower is to walk in the footsteps of the One who is truth.

4. Psychology and the Bible help us to love others well.

Psychology and the Bible work together by building upon key ideas. Examples of how this is done are provided throughout this book. One of the main areas where this occurs is in the area of love. Love is an ongoing theme in the Bible with the word *love* occurring 1,205 times in the Scriptures. In the Bible we learn that:

- Love is important. It is so vital to the Bible story that Jesus proclaimed the entire law and prophets, could be summed up in the message "love God and love other people."[5]
- 1 Corinthians Chapter 13, often referred to as The Love Chapter, poetically depicts what love is. This beautiful passage of Scripture has been recited at countless weddings and provides insights into the power, beauty and mystery of love.
- We learn that "God is love,"[6] and are shown the ultimate example of love, found in Jesus Christ laying down his life for us.[7]

Love is a theme that runs deep throughout the Scriptures. Christ followers possess a burning desire to live out acts of compassion toward others. The Bible ignites a love for humanity in a way that no other book does. But a sincere desire to care for others is not enough. If we fail to understand the intricate details of what it takes to demonstrate love in life's unique situations, our zeal for helping others can end up causing more harm than good.

When caution is not taken, actions intended to help and heal can instead wound and divide. Love is complex. Because of this, loving actions must be individually tailored to the unique needs of those around us. This is where psychology comes into play. As we learn more about how God uniquely designed our human bodies, we are better able to demonstrate true love. Psychology builds upon Biblical teachings by providing practical applications for love in life's unique and complex situations. As we will see, it takes wisdom to love well.

When Acts of Love Go Wrong

I recently witnessed an unfortunate example of love's good intentions gone unbelievably wrong in an episode of *COPS*. In this reality-based television show, camera crews shadow police officers performing their routine duties. In this particular episode, a police officer and pastor were engaged in conversation outside of a rundown hotel. The pastor explained how, a day earlier, a man from the congregation had approached him after the Sunday morning service and requested help for his alcohol addiction. Wanting to help, the pastor had rented a hotel room where this hurting man could sober up. The pastor drove the man to the hotel, prayed for him and assured him that he would return in the morning to provide additional counseling.

Unfortunately, before the pastor returned, this troubled man wandered into the hotel bar and asked the bartender to charge his drinks to the hotel room credit card. Since the pastor had paid for the room, the room was linked to the church credit card. The credit card company quickly recognized the unusual purchase of large quantities of alcohol on a church credit card and reported the card as stolen. The episode ended with the man who had gone to his pastor looking for support being shamefully led away in handcuffs. The pastor looked on in disbelief, shaking his head and denouncing this man, saying he had rejected help and returned to his sin.

At first glance, this may look like the story of a man who sought support for his challenges and later changed his mind. However, those with training in addiction recovery will view this story in a different light. Recovery specialists know that boredom and loneliness are two major triggers of addiction. The man who went to his pastor seeking help was placed in a situation where he was highly unlikely to succeed. Instead of receiving the community support typically provided to those in addiction recovery programs, this man found himself bored and alone. A small hotel room is a less than favorable environment for beginning the recovery process. Left alone with his thoughts, all of the painful memories this man had attempted to drown out with the use of alcohol came at him in full force. As a result, he did what many alcoholics do when faced with a similar situation—he drank.

I can't help but think how much better things could have turned out if this pastor had referred this man to a quality addiction recovery program instead of attempting to provide the support himself. Because he lacked some much needed knowledge, the pastor's attempts at love produced the opposite effect. And if we are going to be honest with ourselves, we will likely have to admit that at times, we have behaved in a similar manner. If we look close enough, most of us can identify times where we sincerely wanted to provide support to others, but in our zeal, we took a ready-fire-aim approach, (as opposed to the much more helpful progression of ready-aim-fire) that resulted in hurting the very people we wanted to help. I know I have been guilty of this. Sincere but misguided attempts at love happen; the goal is to learn from them. In counseling, these misguided attempts to help are referred to as "practicing outside one's scope of competence." Practicing outside one's scope of competence happens when someone has a true desire to help, but does not possess the skills necessary.

In therapy, practicing outside of one's scope of competence is a serious offence. Therapists are required to consult with other well-trained therapists when they don't have the needed skills and training. Competency is equally important for Christians. To love well, Christ followers must acquire both passion and wisdom. Having just one of these is not enough.

When Wisdom and Passion Meet

When it comes to the concept of love, the Bible and psychology complement each other. The Bible lays a foundation of why we should love and psychology provides insights into what specific acts of love look like. Relationships are messy, and knowing the next right thing to do is not always easy. Psychology helps us gain the competency needed to love competently in the midst of muddled circumstances. A few specific examples of areas where psychology provides additional insights into loving well include times when:

- A family member struggles with symptoms of mental illness.
- A teenager is actively rebelling against the house rules.
- We are connected to someone living in a domestic violence situation.
- Someone we love is struggling with a drug or alcohol addiction.
- Someone close to us continues to be in need of money due to a gambling addiction.
- A couple is experiencing ongoing marital conflict.

- A friend actively goes out of his way to hurt us, and then acts like a close friend again a few minutes later without ever addressing the hurt.

Of course, these are only a few of the many situations where discerning the practical applications of love can be especially difficult. There is a fine line between helping someone get better and enabling them, showing tough-love and just being tough, between correcting and nagging, and between appropriate corrective discipline, versus working out our own need for revenge on others. Yes, it takes wisdom to love well.

Perhaps you have found yourself closely connected to someone in one of these situations or one of the thousands of other complex circumstances that life can send our way. I have, and the good news is that there is hope for healing, but it will involve expanding our knowledge and being willing to learn from life's greatest lessons. Both the Bible and psychology have much to say about these types of situations and we will explore many of them in this book as we further examine practical tools from the Bible and psychology for expanding our leadership, growing our relationships, and increasing our overall wellbeing.

Questions for Additional Reflection and Discussion

1. This chapter presented four ways the Bible and psychology work together to complement each other. Psychology and the Bible:

    *   Acknowledge humanity's brokenness.
    *   Are in the restoration business.
    *   Have a high regard for truth.
    *   Provide insights into what it means to love well.

    Did any of these statements come as a surprise to you? Why or why not?

2. Are there any other ways you can think of that the Bible and Psychology complement each other?

3. This chapter looked at practicing outside of the scope of one's competence. Has there been a time in your life when someone attempted to provide you with support with the end result of doing more harm than good? If so, what happened and what could have been done differently to produce a better outcome?

4. In what areas do you need to increase your own scope of competence in order to serve others better? How will you do this?

5. In which areas do you need to increase your scope of competence in order to better take care of yourself? How will you do this?

Two

Wisdom from God and Science

Lessons on Integration

God's glory is on tour in the skies,
God-craft on exhibit across the horizon.
Madame Day holds classes every morning,
Professor Night lectures each evening.

~ Psalm 19:1, *The Message*

Just as art offers a glance into the artist's soul, nature is God's masterpiece, providing a glimpse into the splendor of our Creator.

Science and the Bible complement each other, and the two are inseparable. Witnessing the collision of God and science firsthand is breathtaking. Henry Ward Beecher, a renowned pastor, speaker, and social reformist, who lived during the nineteenth century, stated: "Every artist dips his brush in his own soul, and paints his own nature into his pictures." With artistic brilliance and scientific intricacy, God fashioned His masterpiece of creation. If you have ever paused to gaze upon this handiwork, then you are well aware that our universe reflects His splendor.

My most vivid memory of being stirred by this occurred during my second year of college. After spending the summer working as a camp counselor, four of the other staff and I piled into a six-passenger minivan and embarked on an adventure to Yosemite National Park. During the eight-hour journey from San Diego to Glacier Point — one of the parks well-known highpoints which has a spectacular view — I was engrossed in conversation and paid little attention to our surroundings.

After hours of non-stop travel, our vehicle finally slowed to a halt. Everyone clambered to get out. It had been a cramped, stuffy drive. Outside, the air was crisp and clean. The trees were a vibrant green, towering and majestic. The scent of pine lingered in the air as the gentle breeze softly rustled through the branches overhead. It was pleasant, far more appealing than the outdoor scenery that I was accustomed to.

We began our trek from the parking lot to the scenic overlook, and as we rounded the bend, Half-Dome, El Capitan, and the valley below came into view. Approaching the overlook, I experienced the burst of excitement that comes with peering down a sheer cliff to a forest 3,000 feet below. Toward the west, Yosemite Falls, the world's fifth tallest waterfall, was rushing in full force. I watched in awe as every second 2,400 gallons of water spilled over the edge of the precipice; plummeting a distance equal to the height of Sears Tower, before vanishing into a grove of trees at the bottom. In an instant, this trip had become so much more than pleasant — I was experiencing God's artwork at its finest, and it was breathtaking!

Later that afternoon, the five of us trekked to an open field just below El Capitan, an enormous mass of stone with a steep face that has become a playground for skilled rock climbers from around the world. When evening approached, we stared in admiration as tiny glimmers of light made their appearance on the rock face. Men and women making the multiple-day climb to the top were latching in their sleeping gear and igniting their lanterns in order to do whatever it is rock climbers do before dozing off while suspended hundreds of feet above the earth.

We observed in wonder as the stars emerged on the horizon—first in the form of a few, faint splotches of light, then, within a matter of minutes, the sun fully set, and the sky was enveloped in a flurry of stars that never before seemed so close nor shone more brilliantly. As if on cue, the first shooting star made its appearance— followed by a second, and many more after that.

Ever since this expedition to Yosemite, I have longed to return. I imagine David having a similar encounter with the exquisiteness of God's universe when he wrote:

> *The heavens declare the glory of God; the sky displays his handiwork. Day after day it speaks out; night after night it reveals his greatness. There is no actual speech or word, nor is its voice literally heard. Yet its voice echoes throughout the earth. (Psalm 19:1-4)*

Something magnificent happens inside of us when we stumble upon the wonders of God's creation—His greatness is revealed without a word. During these times, God's existence isn't questioned; it is known, because the echo of His voice is clear. Just as art offers a glance into the artist's soul, nature is God's masterpiece, which provides a glimpse into the splendor of our Creator.

During these flashes of awe and wonder, when the beauty of nature connects us to God in ways never before imagined, when God's creation is manifest in all of its glory, it's easy to forget that we are also beholding moments of pure science. What I witnessed in the open field that evening was not only the majesty of God's creation, but also astronomy, geology, and physics at their finest. Truly, God and science are inseparable.

The Collision of God and Science

The concept of God and science working together may sound foreign at first, but it is true, and don't let anyone convince you otherwise. Popular culture has attempted to create a rift between the Creator and His creation, but the notion of detaching the two is ridiculous. It would be absurd to read about the glories of God's creation in the Bible and never travel outside one's home to experience these wonders firsthand. The Bible is much more than a book to be studied; it is meant to be lived, experienced, handled, and applied. Similarly, it would be equally as absurd to spend thousands of hours exploring God's incredible creation though the means of astronomy, geology, mathematics, physics, and the other sciences without ever turning toward the Creator to gain additional insights into His creation. God and science simply cannot be separated.

When it comes to our personal growth, God's plan is for us to learn through a variety of means. God has made Himself known to us both through His word and through His creation. To give up on either science or the Bible would be to reject one of God's great gifts by casting off wisdom bestowed to us by our Creator. As we will see, the Bible and psychology each offer unique insights into the areas of self-care, love, and leadership. Throughout this book we will see how the two work together to build on key insights, but before diving in; let's first look at some of the unique contributions that the Bible and psychology have to offer.

The Unique Contributions of the Bible

When it comes to examining the greatest lessons of life, careful study of the Bible is essential. There is no other book like it. The Bible provides one-of-a-kind insights into understanding God, ourselves, and the world around us. A number of things distinguish the Bible from all other books. First, the Bible is uniquely written. If you examine the Bible closely, you will see that it is not just a book, but a compilation of 66 books all rolled into one. There are 39 books that make up the Old Testament and 27 books that form the New Testament. These 66 books were written by over 40 different authors from many different walks of life, including:

- David, a shepherd
- Solomon, a king
- Luke, a medical doctor
- Peter and John, who both were fishermen
- Nehemiah, a cupbearer to the king
- Joshua, a military general
- Paul, a religious leader and later, a tentmaker
- Matthew, a tax collector
- Joseph, a high ranking government official

In addition to being written by numerous authors with a broad range of life experiences, the Bible was also written over an extensive period of time. From start to finish, the Bible took approximately 1,500 years to complete. It was written in three different languages: Hebrew, Aramaic, and Greek. And it was written on three different continents: Africa, Asia, and Europe.

The Bible contains a variety of different writing styles, including historical narratives, poetry, parables, songs written to be sung to music, prophetic writings, and apocalyptic literature. Some books of the Bible, such as Philemon, were initially sent as letters to individuals, while books like I and II Thessalonians were originally letters written to the church.

With a multitude of writing styles, the diversity of languages and cultures, plus the lengthy time gap from start to finish, one would expect to find a hodgepodge of stories with conflicting viewpoints and values throughout the book. Instead, the end result is 66 volumes that cooperate and intertwine to reveal the unfolding story of God's redemption of mankind.

The story of redemption begins in the Garden of Eden and ends in a city with the return of Christ. The Bible begins with God's good creation, conveys humanity's separation from God, provides graphic examples of the chaos resulting from this separation, and then dramatically illustrates God's extensive love for humanity through ongoing actions of redemption. God's love culminates with the giving of His Son, Jesus, to die on a cross as a means of bridging this gap and restoring the broken relationship between God and mankind. The Bible concludes with Christ returning to fulfill His promise of bringing healing and restoration to the earth. Each of the 66 books brings fresh insights into this ongoing saga. What is particularly distinctive about the Bible is that we find ourselves in the middle of its ongoing narrative.

The Intersection of God's Story and Ours

In the Bible, God's story and our story intersect. You and I are included in the Biblical narrative. Throughout the Scriptures, God provides us with instructions regarding what we are to do as we await His return. I had a teacher who used to say, "You and I are on spaceship Earth, with a final destination of our good and God's glory."[1] Yes, it sounds a little cheesy and perhaps a little too much likes a phrase from an episode of *Star Trek*. Nevertheless, I like it because it is a good reminder of our limited influence in the world and God's unlimited power. There is no need for concern in regard to where we are headed. Our final destination is secure and no one is capable of hijacking or altering God's plan in any way. We are on "spaceship Earth," traveling on an unalterable course to God's preordained purpose. No amount of money, no king, president, technological advancement, or anything else will prevent God from accomplishing what He has set out to do.

God's script has been written. It is being played out each day, and we have the privilege of being a part of it. You and I live in the paradox of being in a narrative that is both predetermined and flexible. Hero or villain, God has granted us the freedom to partner with Him or to oppose His work on Earth. We can improvise, ad-lib, and choose which role we will take. However, regardless of our decisions, God's story remains the same. In the end, God plans will prevail. The story we find ourselves in is unfolding on a daily basis, whether we like it or not; the only question is whether you and I will accept God's invitation to join Him in carrying out His work on Earth.

Thus, the Bible is distinctive in that it offers principles for living from the creator of life Himself.

The Divine Authorship of the Bible

In addition to providing insight into daily life, the Bible is also a mystery in that parts of it are beyond the scope of our full comprehension. One of these mysteries is contained in the Bible's authorship. While on one hand, the Bible has over 40 different human authors, it would also be just as accurate to say that the Bible has only one author. 2 Timothy 3:16 provides insights into the Divine authorship of Scripture stating, "All scripture is given by inspiration of God." The word *inspiration* in the original Greek language is *theopnuestos*, a compound word comprised of the words *Theos*, translated *God*, and *puneo*, which means *breath* or *wind*. *Theopnuestos* literally translated, means *God-breathed*.

During a hermeneutics class I took during my seminary days, I memorized a definition of inspiration that I am still able to recite to this day. According to my seminary professor, "Inspiration is that quality inherent in the autographs of Scripture that render them as much the word of God as if God had personally breathed them out of his mouth."[2] The Bible is God's word in such a way that, when Scripture speaks, God speaks. The ultimate, unique contribution of Scripture is that it contains the very words of God Himself.

This is why the Bible is absolutely essential to any book looking to examine life's greatest lessons. Without scripture, these lessons would be incomplete. *Coffee Shop Conversations on the Bible and Psychology* is intentionally packed with scripture because life's greatest lessons are connected to the creator of life Himself. In the chapters ahead we will see that many of the principles of psychology have an additional layer of depth that can be added to them when combined with Scriptural principles.

In his book, *Knowing God*, J.I. Packer paints a brilliant picture of the value of Scripture stating, "As it would be cruel to an Amazonian tribesman to fly him to London, put him down without explanation in Trafalgar Square and leave him, as one who knew nothing of English or England, to fend for himself, so we are cruel to ourselves if we try to live in this world without knowing about the God whose world it is and who runs it."[3] Through the Bible we acquire instructions and guidance from the creator of life Himself.

Many excellent books have been written expounding upon the key principles contained in Scripture. Yet very few seek to combine the insights of psychology with the significant teachings of the Bible, and much is lost when principles from psychology are excluded. Let's look at four reasons why integrating psychology and Scripture is valuable.

1. Psychology bridges the time and culture gap.

Timeless principles are just that, timeless. They are effective regardless of the age, place, or culture in which we live. Yet, in order to be effective, these principles must be applied, and this can be difficult when a time and culture gap exists. The life lessons in this book are steady and unchanging, yet the applications of these principles continue to evolve with our ever-developing culture.

Social media provides an excellent example of the need for tools that bridge the culture gap. The importance of fellowship is highlighted throughout Scripture and social media is a recent, cultural phenomenon that has the ability to help or to hinder our fellowship with others. For example:

Ecclesiastes 4:9-12 states:

Two people are better than one, because they can reap more benefit from their labor. For if they fall, one will help his companion up, but pity the person who falls down and has no one to help him up. Furthermore, if two lie down together, they can keep each other warm, but how can one person keep warm by himself? Although an assailant may overpower one person, two can withstand him. Moreover, a three-stranded cord is not quickly broken.

This sound advice is eloquently stated, and in the twenty-first century, we find both new avenues as well as new roadblocks to putting these principles of love and connection into practice. For example, those who use any one of the many social media sites available find themselves inundated with detailed information about the lives of their friends. Through social media, we have the opportunity to view photos of our friends' major life events including weddings, graduations, the birth of children, and family vacations.

Social media also provides glimpses into the minute details of our friends' lives, with some going so far as to post what they ate for lunch, moment by moment updates of how they are feeling throughout the day, and grand announcements of when they decide to work out at the gym. Personally, I have not figured out why people feel the need to post this information, and yet I also find these posts oddly entertaining.

In spite of all of this information about our friends, we may not have face-to-face contact for months, years, or even decades. This cultural change brings up all sorts of questions in regard to what it means to love others and to be connected to them. Questions like:

- How do I love others and cultivate friendships in the midst of a society that is both so connected and disconnected at the same time?
- What does love and connection look like in the Twenty-first century?

- How can I take advantage of these changes to increase my love and deepen my connection to others?
- What are the pitfalls of these cultural changes and how do we avoid them?
- How do these societal changes impact my own mental health and personal wellbeing?

These are a few of the questions that could be asked about the many cultural changes that have recently occurred. Psychology seeks to provide answers to these types of questions. Because psychology continues to develop, it is a tool that is able to support us in integrating timeless principles into our day and culture. Psychology takes into account the unique privileges and stressors of our time. It helps us make the most of new technological advancements and insights. It also helps us to avoid the pitfalls that arise from an ever-evolving society. In short, psychology helps us to bridge the time and culture gap.

2. Psychology takes into account the uniqueness of our personalities and situations.

In addition to bridging the time and culture gap, psychology provides insights for bridging the gap between you, me, and everyone else on the planet. Each one of us is unique. There is no one else alive who is quite like you. Psychologists refer to us as biopsychosocial beings. Each one of us has a distinctive biological, psychological, and social design. Genetic material, thoughts, feelings, and the friends we associate with all work together to make us who we are. I often tell my daughters that they are like snowflakes. Just as there are no two snowflakes exactly alike, there is no one else quite like them, and there is no one just like you. You have been beautifully handcrafted by God.

In Psalm 139:13 David writes,

> *Certainly you made my mind and heart; you wove me together in my mother's womb. I will give you thanks because your deeds are awesome and amazing. You knew me thoroughly...*

God has created each of us as a one-of-a-kind, exclusive individual. As a result, life lessons must be translated to fit our distinctive personalities. Advice that has worked well for others in the past will not necessarily produce similar results for us. The details of our individuality and the specifics of each situation must be taken into account. Psychology strives to bridge this gap in a number of ways. In its search for timeless principles, psychology utilizes both surveys and case studies to gather information from multitudes of people as well as from individuals. Surveys study many people at once in hopes of identifying key principles that are true of us all.

Case studies examine one person at a time, gleaning insights from extraordinary examples, outliers, geniuses, and exceptions to the rules. Through these studies, we see that people are so unique that there are some exceptions to almost every rule.

While many of these exceptions only impact a small percentage of the overall population, these differences are very important to the people who fall into the category of being the exception. For example, the prevalence rate of obsessive-compulsive personality disorder (OCPD) is only one percent.[4] Yet, for that one percent of the population and their loved ones, knowing how to manage the signs and symptoms associated with OCPD is incredibly valuable.

By gleaning insights from the experiences of hundreds of thousands of people, psychology is able to discover wisdom for very specific needs and situations. Life can be messy. What works for one person will not always work for others. Instead of trying harder to force a single strategy to produce results, psychology understands that specific tools and techniques will benefit some individuals more than others. In psychology, strategies are tried out, modified to fit individual needs, and updated with new strategies when better information becomes available, in order to accommodate the unique, God-given makeup of each person.

3. Psychology provides specific applications.

In my work with families, it has been my experience that many people intellectually know what they need to do to overcome the challenges they are facing, but they have difficulty putting the wisdom they have into action. We live in a society where an abundance of sound advice is available, yet people often fail to put it into practice. A while back, I saw a cartoon on social media that made me laugh. It was also a sobering reminder of how often we — myself very much included — fail to make the most of what we already know. In this cartoon, one person asked another, "If we could go back in time 100 years and tell the people of Earth about the future, what do you think they would find most unbelievable?" The answer: "That we have a device that we carry around in our pockets that contains the most up-to-date wisdom and counsel from people all over the world... and most folks use it to look at pictures of kittens and baby owls."[5]

As a therapist and college professor, I found this answer both humorous and humbling. While I like to think that I pass on life-changing advice to the students I teach, the truth is there is very little knowledge I impart that cannot be looked up on the Internet, read in an e-book, or looked up on one's smartphone. We have a wealth of information available at our fingertips. However, if we have trouble applying what we already know, we may find ourselves engaging in trivial activities instead of continuing to grow. It's difficult to motivate ourselves to continue learning when we are already frustrated in our attempts to apply what we know. This is a common challenge. Many people feel incapable of doing the good things they know they should do.

When I find myself feeling stressed and over-whelmed, I can almost always connect these feelings to a basic principle that has been violated. Many times, it's not new knowledge that is needed so much as strategies for applying the wisdom I already have.

James 1:22 says, "But be sure you live out the message and do not merely listen to it and so deceive yourselves." The easy part of change is deciding what we would like to do; the real challenge comes in putting what we know into practice. An armchair quarterback barks out advice to the professionals on-screen. Although the advice might be sound, this man is nowhere near a place of following that advice himself. It takes daily discipline and practice in addition to knowledge to be a professional football quarterback. When it comes to words of wisdom, sometimes we can be more like that armchair quarterback than we like to admit. We give advice we have not yet learned how to follow. It's not that we don't want to follow this advice; it's just that talking is so much easier than doing. Action takes discipline and discipline builds through time and consistency.

This is where psychology helps immensely. Psychology aids us in moving toward doing those things we know we need to get done, one step at a time. Psychology accomplishes this in a number of different ways. Sometimes it breaks down a task into a specific plan of action, other times it provides insights into working smarter and not harder, allowing us to accomplish more in a shorter amount of time and with less effort. Finally, it provides tools for staying motivated, knowing that lasting change occurs over time. Psychology is valuable because it provides specific tools and action steps for putting wise advice into practice on a day-to-day basis.

4. Psychology provides new insights into human behavior, growth, and development.

Timeless principles are great, and so are new insights. We need both. If we only use the tools that we have always had, we will severely limit our growth. Psychology is continually seeking new insights into human behaviors. One example of this is in the increase in focus on positive psychology. Initially, psychology placed an emphasis on all of the things that could go psychologically wrong with a person. The result of this emphasis was the creation of the *Diagnostic and Statistical Manual of Mental Disorders*, the extensive classification of mental disorders mentioned earlier.

A lot of good came out of the *DSM* because it provided a common language for talking about mental illness that led to improved treatment and care. As more and more people sought support, those struggling with signs and symptoms of a diagnosable mental illness began to realize that they were not alone in their struggles. The *DSM* became a tool that brought hope for healing. Nevertheless, the focus was primarily on helping people become less damaged.

Fast-forward to today. In addition to reducing psychological pain, psychology now focuses on positive growth, understanding that people shine when they focus on building on their strengths as opposed to only working on their weakness. Tools like the *Strengths Finder Assessment* help people discover and utilize their top strengths.

Recent studies show that once a person reaches a place where their mind is focused on the positives seventy-five percent of the time or more, as opposed to thinking self-defeating thoughts, a dramatic increase in creativity, productivity, and relational harmony results.[6] Psychology has transformed from a discipline that supports people in lessening their anguish to one that also provides insights into a movement toward excellence, and I believe that the best is yet to come. New insights are being discovered each year that increase our understanding of how to live happy, healthy lives in harmony with others.

Integration for Dynamic Growth

Integration is powerful because it leads to dynamic growth. And as you can see, the Bible and psychology integrate very naturally. One reason for this is that the Bible often prescribes a *what,* while psychology provides a *how.* Often, the Bible tells believers what they should do and psychology provides additional insights into how to accomplish the prescribed task.

A good example of this can be found in 2 Timothy 2:15 where the Apostle Paul exhorts believers to, "Study to shew thyself approved unto God, a workman that needeth not to be ashamed, rightly dividing the word of truth." This verse is taken from the King James Version of the Bible because it includes the word "study." Other translations state to "be diligent"[7] and to "make every effort."[8] The Greek word *spoudazo* means "to exert one's self, endeavor, give diligence."[9] For this specific illustration, we will use the word "study," because it is a clear example of a "what" provided by the Bible. In this verse the Bible is telling believers what to do: we are to diligently study the word of truth.

But how do we accomplish this? We could begin by opening the Bible at random and starting to read, but this would not be the most effective strategy. From psychology we find a multitude of tools for getting the most from our studies. We know that more information is learned, and that information is better retained, when we space our study over time as opposed to attempting to cram in large amounts of information at once. Thus, we will retain information better if we do four, one-hour study sessions over the course of the week than we will if we do one, four-hour study session. We also learn better when we get enough sleep and take care of our bodies through good diet and frequent exercise.

Our physical health impacts our ability to learn and retain new information. Students who stay up all night studying before a big test are learning less effectively than students who study on a daily basis and go to sleep at a reasonable hour. Both types of students are diligently studying; however, the group using tools from psychology will have better results. They are working smarter, not harder. In this example, psychology adds to Biblical insights and helps us to get the most out of our efforts. This is just one of the many examples that could be given. As you can see, and will continue to see throughout this book, when principles from psychology and the Bible are combined, it leads to dynamic growth.

Life Lessons from Psychology and the Bible

At times life is hard. At other times life is fun, funny, and incredibly beautiful. By seeking out wise advice we can make sure the challenging times in life are not more challenging than they need to be, and we can get the most out of the joyful times in life!

Questions for Additional Reflection and Discussion

1. What did you learn from this chapter about the unique contributions of the Bible and psychology to our personal development? Is there anything in this chapter that surprised you or that increased your understanding of the importance of psychology or the Bible in how people grow?

2. Describe the unique contributions of the Bible and the unique contributions of psychology in acquiring wisdom in the areas of leadership, relationships, and life in general?

3. Create a pros and cons list in regard to integrating the Bible with psychology by writing the positives of integration on one side of the paper and the negatives on the other. Overall, do you see the pros of integration outweighing the cons or vice-versa? Why do you believe this?

4. How did you feel about the idea of integrating tools from psychology with Biblical teaching before reading this chapter? How do you feel about it now? Did your opinion about integration change at all and, if so, how?

Three

The Power of Our Thoughts:

Life Lessons from the Cognitive Theories

People don't just get upset. They contribute to their upsetness.

~ Albert Ellis

Angry people stir up a lot of discord;
the intemperate stir up trouble.

~ Proverbs 29:22 *The Message*

Trust the process
~ *Dr. Barry Lord*

When I was in high school our youth pastor told two stories to illustrate how our thoughts influence our feelings and our actions.[1] The first story was about two prisoners who shared the same tiny cell. The conditions were wretched and the men had no contact with the outside world. Each man longed for the day he would be set free. With little to do to occupy their time, the men often found themselves gazing out the one small window in their cell. The first man stared intently at the window bars, and as he stared, frustration and anger welled up inside of him. The bars were a constant reminder of the cage in which he lived. He was trapped, and the more he focused on the bars, the more frustrated he became.

The second prisoner, however, had a much different experience. As he lay in his bunk, he would look past the bars, where he could make out a few faint stars glimmering on the horizon. For this man, the stars symbolized a life beyond the prison walls. They were an ongoing reminder that freedom continued to exist and brought the anticipation of one day beginning a new life. While gazing at those stars, a smile would come across this man's face and hope welled up within him.

Both men stared out of the same window and each longed for freedom, yet one became bitter while the other grew increasingly hopeful. How is it that two men facing similar adversity found themselves having opposite reactions to the same experience? Why did one man become bitter while the other grew increasingly optimistic? The only difference between these two men is where they chose to place their focus. One man honed-in on the bars trapping him, while the other man looked past his painful circumstances and saw the stars. What each man decided to concentrate on made all the difference.

The second story our youth pastor would tell was about a grandfather and his granddaughter who woke up early one morning to walk along the seashore. On this particular day, the tide had washed hundreds of starfish up on the beach. The two were saddened, knowing that the starfish would not survive the afternoon heat. The grandfather continued walking, paying little attention to the starfish. However, the granddaughter would stop as often as she could, pick up a single starfish and gently return it to the sea. She would then run as fast as she could to catch up to her grandfather who had continued his stroll along the shore. She would pick up another starfish and repeat the process of gently returning it to the sea. After watching this go on for some time, the grandfather looked at his granddaughter sadly and said, "There are hundreds of starfish out here, you can't possibly save them all and you'll wear yourself out trying. Why don't you stop?" The little girl looked at her grandfather with a smile and replied, "I know I can't save them all, but what I'm doing matters to this one." Then she picked up another starfish, walked down to the ocean and gently placed it back in.

I don't know if either of these stories are true, but I like them because they demonstrate the power of our thoughts and beliefs. The first story illustrates how the thoughts we think impact how we feel. If we attend to the "bars," or negative events in life, we will find ourselves, day by day, becoming increasingly frustrated. On the other hand, if we choose to look past the "bars" and focus on life's "stars," we will fill up with hope as we concentrate on the bright possibilities ahead.

The second story demonstrates how our beliefs influence our actions. For example, if we truly believe the world is a dangerous place where people are quick to take advantage of us, and that no one will look out for us so we must look out for ourselves, we will back up those beliefs with certain types of actions. These core beliefs will result in us becoming guarded, suspicious of others, hyper-vigilant, and aloof. On the other hand, if our core beliefs are that the world is generally a safe place where others are trustworthy and willing to support us during our times of need, we will act in a far different manner. These types of beliefs allow us to confidently connect to others and assertively ask for support when we need it. How we feel moment by moment and the actions we take throughout the day are strongly related to the thoughts we think and the core beliefs we hold.

The Discovery of the Cognitive Therapies

This chapter focuses on two specific cognitive therapies — rational emotive behavioral therapy, also known as REBT, established by Albert Ellis; and cognitive behavioral therapy, or CBT, developed by Aaron Beck. Both were formulated during the 1950's and 1960's and have similar, foundational concepts. Ellis and Beck both understood the power that our thoughts and beliefs have in influencing our feelings and behaviors. Yet, the two therapeutic modalities have distinctive techniques.

Albert Ellis

Albert Ellis' story is a tribute to the effectiveness of REBT. He is a man who lived out the core teachings that he later imparted to others. Albert was born in Pittsburg, Pennsylvania, on September 27, 1913 and faced a number of challenges that began in childhood. Between the ages of five and seven, he was continually in and out of the hospital due to a variety of illnesses. Albert's parents would go on to have two more children and, as the oldest sibling, Albert was put in charge of caring for his younger brother and sister while his parents worked. Ellis described his parents as emotionally distant, and he was painfully shy. Albert was in the midst of his teenage years when the Great Depression struck, and he found a job to help support his family during this time. All of this is significant because, in spite of a socially and economically disadvantaged childhood, Ellis would go on to become one of the most influential psychotherapists in history. He had such an ability to connect with people that *Psychology Today* referred to him as the "average living psychologist," a title that emphasizes his wisdom, humanity, and ability to connect with others.

Albert Ellis was a man who lived what he taught. He grew up with his own social anxieties and worked to overcome them. As a teenager, young Albert once forced himself to talk to 100 women in a local park over a period of a few months in order to desensitize himself to his fear of rejection.

Years later, Dr. Ellis would encourage his clients to engage in shame attacking exercises that involved a similar emotional risk of a shy teenager forcing himself to converse with women he didn't know. In these experiments, clients were encouraged to act in safe yet socially inappropriate ways in order to test the reality of their fears. Specific examples of these experiments included facing the social awkwardness of stopping a bus only to decide not to get off and asking to buy tobacco in a hardware store. These events, though mildly embarrassing, did not produce the disastrous results the clients feared, and they created teachable moments where each client discovered that his or her dreaded embarrassment was easily forgiven. People who had built up overly dramatic scenarios in their head had their anxieties eased as they faced their inner demons and discovered that afterwards life progressed as normal. Ellis believed that people have a natural tendency to disturb themselves, and the ability to make themselves happy. He wrote,

> *"If you are disturbed, you largely make yourself that way — you create your self-defeating behaviors... You do not passively get or become upset. No, you largely consciously and un-consciously manufacture your own disturbances. And, you will see, that's good. Yes! Because if you make yourself upset, you usually have the ability and power to act less stupidly and to unupset yourself."*[2]

As you can see, Albert Ellis was brazen and straightforward in his approach. His techniques are empowering, and show us that because we cause many of our own disturbances, we have the power to uncause them. He was a man who provided people with specific action steps for looking past the "bars" in life to discover the bright, shining "stars."

Aaron Beck

Aaron Beck was born on July 18, 1921. He worked as a psychologist and college professor and came to be known as, The Father of Cognitive Therapy. Similar to Ellis, Beck's work also focuses on the connections between thoughts and feelings. Beck taught his clients about the cognitive triad which consists of negative thoughts about one's self, the world around them, and the future. Negative thoughts, if dwelt on long enough, will lead to decreased energy, lower mood, and maladaptive behaviors that snowball to form the symptoms of depression. Beck taught that it is not our experiences, but our interpretation of our experiences that determines our mood. He once wrote, "Whether or not the person experiences pleasure depends on the meaning attached to a particular situation or object." Like rational emotive behavioral therapy, cognitive behavioral therapy is empowering because it demonstrates that we have much control over our own happiness and unhappiness.

Today, skills from cognitive therapy are taught by therapists, life coaches, pastors, mentors, and personal trainers, in a variety of settings. These tools have a broad range of application and are used to help people overcome symptoms of depression and anxiety, in addition to assisting people in attaining higher levels of leadership and personal success. CBT tools are widely used because of their verified effectiveness and ease of use.

Cognitive Behavioral Therapy and the Bible

Many years before the tools and techniques of CBT and REBT were formalized by psychologists, the key concepts of these theories were inscribed in the Scriptures. One of the greatest stories illustrating the ability of thoughts and beliefs to impact emotions and actions can be found in Acts, Chapter 5.

The story begins with the Apostles being forcefully brought before the Sanhedrin, the official religious court of the day. The Apostles had been previously warned not to teach about Jesus, to which Peter replied, "We must obey God rather than people" (Acts 5:29). Seeing that the Apostles continued to disregard their religious rules, the officials sternly warned them a second time before having them flogged to emphasize their point. It would have been natural for the Apostles to become discouraged, and completely understandable for them to have doubts about continuing the life of an Apostle. After all, the only thing they were guilty of was doing exactly what

Apostles were commanded to do: they were telling others about Jesus.

Getting flogged for doing one's job provides a perfect excuse for wallowing in self-pity. The Apostles could have viewed the flogging as a horrible event and even viewed it as a sign of personal failure, but none of this happened. Instead, the beating produced the opposite effect. One might say the Apostles saw stars instead of bars, but it would be more accurate to say that they heard the praise of their Master instead of feeling the sting of the whip. The Bible states that the Apostles began rejoicing and praising God, celebrating that they were counted worthy to suffer for the cause of Christ. The beating that was meant to cause pain and shame was worn as a badge of honor and as a direct result of their optimistic outlook; the Apostles became increasingly fired up about spreading the good news of salvation through Jesus Christ. This historic event is a demonstration of cognitive therapies at their best!

Thoughts and the Bible

The Apostles held the core belief that pleasing God was far more important than keeping the religious leaders happy, and these fundamental values fueled their actions. What we believe is important because it heavily influences the actions that we take. God designed us to function this way and the value of thoughts and beliefs is a theme that runs deep throughout Scriptures. Some of the many passages that touch on this theme include:

- *Philippians 4:8* Finally, brothers and sisters, whatever is true, whatever is worthy of respect, whatever is just, whatever is pure, whatever is lovely, whatever is commendable, if something is excellent or praiseworthy, think about these things (NET).
- *Romans 8:6* For the outlook of the flesh is death, but the outlook of the Spirit is life and peace.
- *Proverbs 23:7* For as he thinketh in his heart, so *is* he (KJV).
- *2 Timothy 1:7* For God hath not given us the spirit of fear; but of power, and of love, and of a sound mind (NIV) (God's desire is that we be sound-minded).
- *Isaiah 26:3* You will keep him in perfect peace, whose mind is stayed on you: because he trusts in you (NIV).
- *Romans 12:2* Do not be conformed to this present world, but be transformed by the renewing of your mind (NET).

As you can see, where we choose to focus our attention is important. In the Bible, God calls people to be aware of their thoughts and to put sound-minded thinking into practice.

Putting the Cognitive Therapies to Work

When I began the counseling program at Southern California Seminary, our dean, Dr. Barry Lord, used to repeat the phrase, "Trust the process," over and over again. It was his way of encouraging our class to lay aside our fears, frustrations, and protests about trying new ways of doing things. It was a request to progress through the program without arguing; trusting that in the end, the effort we put forth would transform us into well-trained therapists. For many of us, "Trust the process" became an empowering mantra propelling us forward.

For me personally, whenever there was an assignment I didn't want to complete, and during the times that I felt nervous and doubted my own competence, the words "Trust the process" would pop into my head. What's funny is that these words would enter my thoughts with the exact same tone and inflection used by our dean when he would speak them. He had literally gotten inside of my head. And it worked! These words motivated me to lay aside my fears, doubts, and protests. I chose to move forward and, as a result, graduated from the program.

Self-Talk

The phrase "Trust the process" is an example of a positive self-talk. Learning to monitor and change self-talk is an especially useful tool from the cognitive therapies because it's a tool that can be used by anyone and applied to almost every situation. Whether we are aware of it or not, all of us have a running dialogue going on inside of our head. Therapists refer to this dialogue as self-talk, because in these conversations we are telling ourselves how to feel about the events going on around us. Negative self-talk statements drag us down. They decrease our energy level, raise our anxiety, and hold us back from doing things we would like to do.

On the other hand, positive self-talk is empowering, energizing, and motivates us to move forward. Positive self-talk is what allows people to push forward to accomplish their dreams in spite of the roadblocks in front of them. Let's look at how changing one's self-talk from negative to positive works.

The first steps in altering self-talk involve increasing our ability to recognize when self-talk is occurring and then identifying whether the dialog is helpful or harmful. One way to increase awareness of your self-talk is to pause when you find yourself experiencing strong emotions. Intense feelings of happiness, sadness, and frustration are all signals that self-talk is taking place. During times of strong emotion, take a moment to see if you can identify the specific thoughts going through your mind. You will likely discover that your brain is subtly telling your body what to feel about the situation.

If you find that you are feeling bad, it might because you are using negative self-talk phrases that resemble the following:

- "This is awful."
- "This is catastrophic."
- "I should, must or have to..."
- "I am a failure."
- "I will always fail."

Albert Ellis referred to this type of disempowering self-talk as "awefulizing" and "catastrophizing." Awefulizing and catastrophizing are two ways people magnify the negative events around them. To engage in this type of self-talk is to make a mountain out of a mole-hill, and to attempt to make lemons out of lemonade. Yes, this is technically impossible, but CBT therapists recognize that people can be funny creatures who at times, go to great lengths to disturb themselves.

Cognitive therapists discourage the use of self-talk that includes the language "I should," "I must," and "I have to," because it adds undue pressure to succeed. The well-known psychoanalyst Karen Horney was so strongly opposed to these types of self-commands that she coined the term "the tyranny of the shoulds." Instead, language such as "I would prefer," and "It would be nice if..." is encouraged because it acknowledges that there is an ideal outcome for the situation while also inferring that, if this outcome is not achieved, it is not truly disastrous.

Two additional strategies included in self-sabotaging self-talk include personalization and globalization. In personalization, events are internalized, and in globalization, a single event is used as a defining moment to predict the outcome of all future events. To further explain, imagine for a moment that you have just failed a major test. You could personalize that failure by telling yourself, "I'm a failure." Next, you could then increase your misery by globalizing the failure and telling yourself, "There is no use in trying again, because I will always fail." This type of thinking is obviously irrational and, hopefully, you can easily identify the errors. Failing one test hardly makes anyone a failure and it is certainly not a predictor of things to come. Possible alternatives to these negative self-talk statements include, "I failed this time. Next time I will spend more time studying and will do better..." and, "This is an opportunity to learn better study habits."

While it's often easy to recognize unreasonable thinking in others, irrational beliefs can be sneaky. They tend to creep into our minds and lay down roots before we are aware of what has happened. REBT teaches us to dispute our irrational beliefs and CBT provides a model for replacing negative self-talk statements with positive ones. Let's look at both.

Disputing Irrational Beliefs

Disputing irrational beliefs involves asking ourselves, "What is the proof? Where is the evidence for this?" If we rationally analyze the situations we are viewing as awful and catastrophic, most often we will have to admit that, in reality, these events are really only sad, disappointing, or frustrating. Changing our self-talk from "This is awful..." (or whatever words you use to magnify the event in your own self-talk) to "This is disappointing..." diminishes the power given to the event. The goal of REBT is not to engage in a form of extreme, positive psychology that naively ignores life's challenges; there is no need to try to convince yourself that life is all rainbows and unicorns... it's not. But it's not all despair and gloom, either. Rational beliefs are just that, rational and acting rationally means neither overreacting nor underreacting to the circumstances around us.

According to cognitive therapists, negative emotions such as anger, sadness, and frustration are not bad. Each of these emotions serves a purpose. For example, grief is good for a time because it acknowledges that a loss has taken place and allows us to move through our pain. But grieving a loss is far different from wallowing in misery. The difference is that grief is a process wherein people progress though stages of sorrow to arrive healthier and happier on the other side. On the other hand, wallowing in self-pity has no process. Instead, the person either remains stagnant, or sinks ever deeper into an ocean of despair. The good news is that Christ followers have powerful tools for regaining momentum during times of loss. The Bible provides the ultimate REBT tools... or REBT on steroids, so to speak.

Romans 8:28 says, "And we know that all things work together for good for those who love God, who are called according to his purpose." According to this passage, it is impossible for any event to be truly catastrophic because God is always in control. No matter how bad events may appear, God is continually working all things for our good and His glory. Although bad things do happen, all of these events are in the hands of our loving Heavenly Father. The only rational response to this is to mourn our losses and to rejoice in God's goodness. Times of sorrow never have to end in despair. Because of who God is, we have hope!

Learning to focus on life's stars is an extremely valuable skill. Because we are biopsychosocial beings, the types of thoughts we think seep into every aspect of our life and directly impact our biology and relationships.

When Our "Thinking Brain" Shuts Down

Neuroscience shows that, in times of crisis, the critical thinking part of our brain shuts down, and there is no better way to work ourselves into a frantic state than to convince ourselves that we *should, must,* and *absolutely have to* accomplish a given task. We can continue to add fuel to this fire by telling ourselves these tasks *have to* be accomplished *right now!*

When we build up this heightened since of urgency in our minds, we activate a very small part of our brain called the amygdala. This almond-sized portion of our brain is an emergency response system that initiates our body's fight, flight, or freeze responses. The amygdala is a God-given defense mechanism that propels us into action. It can be a life-saver during times of crisis. The amygdala is what causes us to rapidly swerve out of the way of an oncoming driver who recklessly forces himself into our lane. It causes us to rush into action if a house catches on fire and when our children are in danger. However, the amygdala can also create chaos in relationships. While the amygdala pushes us to act, it also shuts off the frontal cortex, or critical thinking part of the brain. This is the part of our brain that is needed to successfully resolve relational conflicts.

Perhaps you have driven down a country road late at night when suddenly a deer bolted in front of your car. Likely, as a result of seeing the deer, you either slammed on the car's brakes or took quick, evasive actions to swerve out of the way. These types of reactions are examples of the amygdala's beneficial aspects — the fight, flight and freeze responses that help keep us safe from harm.

On the other hand, an example of the amygdala's detriments is seen in the deer's reaction to the presence of the car. When a deer sees a set of headlights heading in its direction, the deer may bolt in a wild frenzy. In certain situations, this defense mechanism is useful for keeping the animal safe from predators. The only problem is that, with the thinking part of the brain shut down, the deer may make the unfortunate mistake of bolting in front of the car instead of avoiding it.

Like a deer in the headlights, when our amygdala is triggered we often find ourselves saying and doing things we later regret. By monitoring our self-talk, we can stop this tiny part of our brain from becoming unnecessarily activated.

What to Say When Talking to Ourselves

Thus far, we have looked at reducing the impact of negative emotions by disputing irrational beliefs. The next step is to add in positive self-talk. This is where the use of these tools really gets exciting because it shows us how to add energy and positive momentum into our life. Positive self-talk is a tool that David used on a consistent basis and can be seen throughout the Psalms, many of which were composed by him. 1 Samuel 30:6 recounts a challenging time in David's life. Although he began by being upset, "David drew strength from the Lord his God." This is something that David practiced doing throughout his lifetime.

It is not uncommon for a psalm to begin with sorrow and end in rejoicing. Initially, the focus of these psalms is on the surrounding negative circumstance. Then a gradual progression of focusing on God's power, goodness, and willingness to intervene takes place. Like David, we can change our self-talk by taking our focus off the negative aspect of the situation and placing it on God's goodness. Few events are black-and-white. There is truth in the well-used phrase, "Even dark clouds have a silver lining." There is a time to mourn over life's lemons and a time to take those same lemons and make them into lemonade.

To find the positives in the midst of challenging circumstances, we can ask the following questions:

- What is good about this situation?
- What new opportunities does this challenge create?
- What can I learn from this experience?
- How can this event help me to learn and grow?
- Are there ways I can use this situation to my advantage?
- How is God working in the midst of this trial?
- What might God want me to learn from this?
- How is this challenge deepening my relationship with God and with other people?

You can use the answers to these questions to create new self-talk phrases. Then, when you catch yourself engaging in negative self-talk, you can change your self-talk to your pre-determined phrase. You can also use these phrases to keep you motivated and energized throughout the day. Yes, it sounds simple and may feel a little uncomfortable at first, but it works.

Another option to creating self-talk statements is to memorize key passages of Scripture and meditate on them throughout the day. When you catch yourself engaged in negative self-talk, you can then pause for a moment, stop the negative self-talk, and replace those thoughts with either a positive self-talk statement or a specific scripture. Let's look at some examples of negative self-talk and ways that positive alternatives and scriptural truths can be used to replace these destructive thought patterns:

- Negative self-talk: "I'm a failure."
- Positive alternative: "I failed this time, but will learn from this experience and will do better next time."
- Scriptural truth: "I'm a son/daughter of God" (1 John 3:1).

- Negative self-talk: "This is awful."
- Positive alternative: "This is really disappointing."
- Scriptural truth: "God is willing and able to take this bad situation and work it for my good and His glory" (Romans 8:28).

Another tool similar to monitoring self-talk involves reframing the way we think about the events that happen to us. Like a painting that is taken out of an old, tattered frame and re-framed in a new one, we have the ability to replace negative perceptions of the world around us with positive alternatives.

Let's look at some specific examples of how reframing works. This time we'll start by looking at the life event, a negative frame that can be placed around this event, an alternative, positive reframe and, finally, a scriptural reframe.

- Event: An argument with a family member or close friend.
- Negative frame: "This is *awful*. I *shouldn't* argue with others."
- Positive reframe: "This is an opportunity to learn new relationship skills, deepen our bond, and to work through some longstanding challenges."
- Scriptural reframe: "This is an opportunity to put Romans 12:18 into practice and learn to live at peace with others."

- Event: The death of a loved one.
- Negative frame: Death is seen as bad, final, and an event that *should not* happen.
- Positive reframe: Death becomes a graduation and a relief from physical suffering.
- Scriptural reframe: "To be absent from the body is to be present with the Lord" (2 Corinthians 5:8, paraphrased).

When losses occur and things don't work out as planned, utilizing positive self-talk and reframes can help us move through the stages of grief and assist us in regaining positive momentum in our lives. When things are going well, these tools help us to maintain momentum, keep us motivated and assist us in pressing forward with determination and purpose.

Living with the Goal in Mind

In 2 Corinthians 6:4-10, the Apostle Paul presents a beautiful and powerful reframe of his circumstances, stating:

> *But as God's servants, we have commended ourselves in every way... through glory and dishonor, through slander and praise; regarded as impostors, and yet true; as unknown, and yet well-known; as dying and yet – see! – we continue to live; as those who are scourged and yet not executed; as sorrowful, but always rejoicing, as poor, but making many rich, as having nothing, and yet possessing everything.*

For Paul, living the life God called him to was an ongoing adventure. The painful times paled in comparison to the rewards of fulfilling God's purpose in his life. At times life is hard, yet during the difficult times there are always reasons to rejoice. Though it can be challenging to see from the vantage point of pain, years later we often realize that life's struggles contributed the most to our growth.

Experiencing discomfort in growth is normal — working out at the gym results in the aches and pains of new muscle development, children going through a growth spurt know the uncomfortable feeling of growing pains that are a natural part of moving toward maturity, and I would imagine that baby birds who are pushed out of the nest by their mothers experience sheer terror moments before discovering the exhilaration of taking flight.

It is the same with us: often the most painful moments in life lead to the greatest joys. Though hard, life's challenges do not have to be miserable, awful, or catastrophic, and they do not need to prevent us from making our goals a reality. One of life's greatest lessons from the Bible and psychology is that we can choose to take proactive steps to change the way we think, which will, in turn, alter the way we feel and act. As the Bible says, to be spiritually minded truly is "life and peace!"

Life Lessons from the Cognitive Therapies

Our thoughts influence the way we feel and the actions we take. Choose to focus on things that are energizing, motivating, and in alignment with God's word. Then take proactive steps to move toward those goals.

Questions for Additional Reflection and Discussion

1. Are there any current circumstances where you are choosing to see the 'bars' instead of the 'stars' in your life? What would it look like to focus on the positives in these situations?

2. Is there any positive self-talk that you are using on a consistent basis? If not, why not, and what would it look like for you to live out Philippians 4:8 on a daily basis?

3. Is there any negative self-talk that you need to stop dwelling on? If so, what thoughts will you use to replace the negative self-talk?

4. As you read this chapter, did you recognize any irrational beliefs that you are currently holding? How would you dispute these irrational beliefs?

5. What challenge you are currently facing and how could you reframe your self-talk to improve the way you think and feel about that challenge? How could this difficulty be viewed as an opportunity?

6. Are there any Scriptures in this chapter that caught your attention? If so, why do you think this particular passage stood out as especially meaningful?

Four

Finding Freedom in Choices:

Life Lessons from Choice Theory

It is almost impossible for anyone to continue to choose
misery after becoming aware that it is a choice.

~ William Glasser

Wise choices, made over time, generate momentum and magnify positive results.

"Just worry about yourself and not what anyone else in the class is doing." These words were seared into my brain by a wise and somewhat exasperated first-grade teacher. This became our teacher's go-to phrase that she would repeat throughout the day. A student would complain, "...but she gets to write on the chalkboard, why don't I?" and like a broken record, our teacher would respond, "Just worry about yourself and not what anyone else in the class is doing." Another student would bring to the class's attention that there were children playing outside, and reason that, since other children were playing, we should be allowed a similar privilege. This would again result in our teacher, once again, implementing her famous phrase.

As kindergarteners we had discovered that we could avoid our teacher's request to participate in the lesson by stating, "...but she's not paying attention, either..." while pointing out another distracted student nearby. During our preschool and kindergarten years we became experts at focusing the teacher's attention on others. We also saw that we could use a similar technique to manipulate the teacher into allowing us to do activities we wanted. For example, if we saw another student doing something we wanted to do too, we might state, "It's not fair: Johnny is doing art; I want to color, too!" Or we might ask, "But Susie gets to play with the blocks, why can't I?" It was irrefutable kindergarten logic. The only problem is that we were not in kindergarten anymore, and not only had our teacher heard this all before... she was well prepared.

With one simple phrase, our first-grade teacher halted attempts to redirect her attention to others and put an end to our attempts at debate. Over and over again, she would repeat that dreadful phrase, "Yes, you're right, but just worry about yourself and not what anyone else is doing." This statement left our class confounded. The teacher would agree with us and redirect us back to the task at hand. "How do you argue with someone who starts off by telling you 'You're right,'" we wondered?

I'm curious as to whether our teacher knew that in addition to helping us to focus on our work; she was also teaching us foundational concepts of choice theory. While choice theory contains numerous complexities, the key concept of focusing on the choices we can make, as opposed to attempting to control the actions of others, is simple enough to be taught to children in grade school.

Choice Theory Basics

Choice theory was developed by Dr. William Glasser, who began formulating his ideas in the 1960s. His work evolved over the years, initially being called 'reality therapy' in the 1960s and 'control theory' in the 1970s. The name was finally changed to 'choice theory' in 1996. Choice theory first and foremost emphasizes the importance of having close connections to others. It asserts that happy, healthy, productive lives are the result of having positive relationships. As its name suggests, the concept of personal choice is heavily emphasized, and Glasser demonstrates how focusing on the positive choices we can make increases the likelihood of having positive, lasting relationships.

Choice theory asserts that we are where we are in our life and relationships because of the choices we make. If we don't like our current situation, we have the power to change it by choosing differently. However, problems arise when we decide not to focus on the many options available to us, and instead, like grade-school children, try to get what we want with attempts to control the actions of others. Efforts to gain control over others can come in the form of manipulation, bribes, passive-aggressive behaviors, arguing, debating, and throwing temper tantrums, as well as through physical and verbal threats.

Choice theory refers to attempts to control others as *external control psychology*. The heart of choice theory is focusing on the choices we can make as opposed to resorting to techniques from external control psychology (i.e. trying to coerce someone into doing something they do not want to do). External control psychology is seen as extremely damaging because it always, always, always harms the relationship.

Because relationships are held in the highest esteem, external control psychology techniques are shunned. Even if these techniques lead to our desired outcome, the relationship becomes damaged in the process, and getting others to do what we want them to do is not worth the cost of harming the relationship. In his book *Choice Theory*, William Glasser states, "As long as we continue to believe that we can control others or, conversely, that others can control us, the misery associated with common situations such as these will continue unabated."[1]

What "common situations" is Glasser referring to? He's writing specifically about times when:

1. We make attempts to get others to do something they do not want to do through the use of arguments, threats, bribes, and rewards.
2. Someone else attempts to get us to do something that we don't want to do by using similar strategies.
3. We become engaged in a verbal tug-of-war where two people are each trying to convince the other to do something neither of them wants to do.

In short, choice theory is about meeting people where they are at instead of insisting on change. This therapeutic model is especially noteworthy because it has a unique hypothesis about mental illness. It proposes that people do the best they know how to do with the tools they have available. When people don't know what to do, they may choose — yes, choose — to take on the signs and symptoms associated with the *DSM* disorders as a way of coping with their distress. Thus, in choice theory, mental disorders are not considered brain disorders but unconscious choices people make in order to manage relational stress.

According to choice theory, a person is not depressed, but is instead *depressing* or choosing to depress. A person would not have an anxiety disorder, but would be described as *anxieting*. On one hand, this way of thinking about mental health is controversial and should be approached with caution. On the other hand, it is also empowering because, if we are the ones causing our problems, then we also have the power to resolve them.

However, a quick word of caution is necessary here. The idea that a person chooses their symptoms should never be used to demand change. Remember, demands are not consistent with choice theory, but reflect the use of external control psychology. If you find yourself wanting to help someone close to you, and choice theory resonates with you, you might want to ask this person to see someone well trained in this therapeutic modality.

You could even offer to attend the first session with them in order to cheer them on and show your support.

Freedom in Choices

Choice theory reminds us of the incredible freedom we have to make positive choices that improve the situations around us. Like a tiny snowball that rolls down a hill, accumulating snow, gaining mass and eventually setting off an avalanche, the hundreds of seemingly insignificant decisions we make on a daily basis build over time to create a colossal impact on our lives. Some examples of these small choices that build over time include:

- The types of foods that we put into our bodies.
- Choosing to exercise or not exercise.
- Deciding whom we spend time with and how much time we will spend with them.
- The types of books we read.
- The decision to attend or not to attend school, as well as how much time, energy, and effort we will put into each of the classes we take.
- The career we decide on and how much time we devote to our chosen field.
- The decision to get married, stay married, and the amount of emotional investment we pour into this relationship.

These are just a few examples of the multitude of choices readily available to us on a daily basis. It's these seemingly insignificant decisions in life, the ones that we make with hardly a thought, that build over time and impact our lives the most. We have more power than we realize.

According to choice theory, if we don't like the place we are at in life, we have the ability to make different choices and alter our situation. As the old saying goes, "If you always do what you've always done, you'll always get what you've always got." But if we do something different, we will generate different results. We actively create our circumstances and we can actively change them. We have the freedom to choose.

Making the Most of What We Have

At this point, you may be nodding your head in agreement, or perhaps you find yourself protesting in frustration, asserting that you did not get to choose your:

- Parents
- When and where you were born
- What school you attended as a child
- Your IQ and the genes you were given
- Instances of abuse or neglect that happened in childhood, and
- Your physical health, or lack of it

If you find yourself objecting to this idea of freedom by pointing out that some circumstances are beyond your control, you are absolutely right. As nice as it would be to have complete freedom, it's true that we do not have control over everything and children are especially limited in their power. As a child, we did not get to pick our family of origin, or the home that we grew up in. Adults had the ability to tell us what to do and found ways to motivate us to do what they asked of us.

When we became adults, our ability to choose expanded, though if we search long enough; it's likely that we will still find a multitude of areas where this freedom is limited. Even though we do not have complete control, there is always some ability to choose, and this ability to decide what we will do with what we have been given makes all the difference. If we truly believe that we were not given the tools for a good start, it is also true that there have been many people who got off to a slow start and went on to accomplish much in spite of having started their journey with little.

Choice theory acknowledges that we do not get to choose everything. Life is not fair and the playing field is not always level. Some people are born with greater advantages than others. That is reality. Yet choice theory recognizes that the choices we can make are sufficient. When we choose to make the most of what we have by taking consistent, positive action over time, our good choices build to produce powerful results.

William Glasser states, "Happiness or mental health is enjoying the life you are choosing to live, getting along well with the people near and dear to you, doing something with your life you believe is worthwhile, and not doing anything to deprive anyone else of the same chance for happiness you have."[2] All of us have this type of happiness available to us, but it's up to us to make the day-by-day choices that create this reality. We have to choose to do the work necessary to get to where we want to go.

Choosing to Make the Most of What We Have

The idea of choosing to make the most of what we have is illustrated in a parable Jesus told in Matthew 25:14-30. The story is about a wealthy man who, before departing on a long journey, divided his wealth among his servants, giving them the responsibility to invest his finances while he was away. The money he entrusted to each servant was given in the form of a *talent*. A *talent* is a specific weight of silver that, according to historians, was worth about nine years of skilled labor. In modern-day wages, this would translate to approximately $400,000 a very large sum of money![3]

The master of the house was a tremendously wealthy man who had multiple talents to invest. He divided up his savings amongst three of his servants. Today, this would be similar to entrusting one's wealth to competent and experienced investors. The master delegated five talents, or nearly two million dollars, to his wisest, most faithful servant. To the second servant he entrusted two talents, and the master gave one talent to the third, perhaps the intern of the group. The first two servants chose to take full advantage of this opportunity. They invested what they were given, and through hard work and wise investments, were able to double their master's money. However, the third servant became anxious. Fearing that he would make a mistake and lose some of his master's hard-earned wealth, he dug a hole and buried his talent deep in the earth.

When the master returned, he was pleased to find that the servant he delegated five talents to had made wise investments and doubled his money. In a similar manner, the servant who had been entrusted with two talents now had four. But for the servant who had one talent, it was a different story. This servant did not do well in his internship. Uncovering his talent from where it had been hidden, he returned it to his master. I imagine the master of the house shook his head in disbelief. If this servant had only put the money in the bank, it would have at least yielded some interest. The master immediately fired this man from his investment team, taking away the talent he was responsible for and giving it to the servant who had ten.

When I first read this parable, part of me felt sad for the servant who was fired from his job. Certainly this was a major blow for this man. But what about the people who heard this parable—how would they have reacted? At the time this story was told, being a servant meant having limited power. Servants were often delegated the difficult, dirty jobs no one else wanted to do. To be a hired servant put in charge of managing a small fortune would have been a tremendous honor. Not just anyone gets to manage a $400,000 investment. Could you imagine what it would be like to be the master of this house and return to find that your investor put your money in a hole in the ground? Not a bank, not the stock market, but this man actually had the nerve to take a shovel, dig into the earth, and bury his master's hard-earned money. The servant was being paid to invest this money and instead hid it in a place where it would earn no interest, and could easily be dug up and stolen. I don't know about you, but if this servant had been someone that I entrusted with my estate, I would have been furious!

Perhaps the reason I initially felt sorry for this servant is that, at times, I can relate to him. In fact, most of us are like all three servants in the parable at different times in our lives. Like these servants, each of us has been entrusted with talents given to us by God. Not talents of silver as in this parable, but with talents in the form of strengths and resources. Like the servants who were entrusted with money by their master, we too are neither able to decide how many talents we receive nor the specific talents bestowed upon us. But we do have the responsibility of deciding how we will invest what we have been given. In some areas of life we have been given much. Perhaps we have been blessed with good health, were born into a wealthy family, are artistic, or are especially good at sports. These are our five-talent areas. In other areas, we are less talented but still have some strength. These could be considered our one and two-talent areas.

Although we don't get to decide what talents we are given, we do get to choose what we will do with these gifts. We can invest what we have been entrusted with or bury our talents deep down inside. Each of us has talent on loan from God. He has provided us with gifts to invest, and choice theory reminds us that, no matter where we are in life, we can do much with what we have been given.

Putting Our Talents to Work

What I like about this parable is that the master based his response on how well each servant invested the talents he initially received and not on the total amount of money returned. The master was pleased with the servant who had ten talents and the servant who had four. Both had doubled their initial investment and both were honored. The servant who was given two talents was not expected to have finished with ten and it's reasonable to expect that if the servant who had been entrusted with one talent had turned it into two, he would have been equally honored. Like the servants in the parable, we have the freedom to invest and multiply the many talents we have been given. Here are five key principles for making wise investments:

1. Discover your strengths, and put them to work.

Research reveals that we are most successful when we build on our strengths as opposed to spending large amounts of time trying to overcome weaknesses. The once popular advice to build upon weaknesses until they turn into strengths sounds nice, but has proven to be impractical. Each of us has areas where we will excel and other areas where we will always have limited success no matter how hard we try. More is accomplished in less time when our strengths become our primary areas of focus. This is contrary to the popular American ideology that anyone can grow up to be and do anything they set their mind to. While this type of thinking sounds nice, it is not in alignment with reality. God has given us our gifts for a reason and we thrive when we focus on the talents that He has bestowed upon us.

This is a lesson I learned the hard way. At one point in my life I extensively studied music. I took private guitar lessons and signed up for music theory classes in college. I practiced playing in the background at summer camp and during our children's worship service at church. After months of practice the opportunity to lead worship

119

on my own finally arrived. My audience was a Sunday school class consisting of about twenty first-grade children. I stood before the class, confident, with guitar in hand. I reviewed the words and hand motions to the song and began leading the class in a time of worship. What happened next was a powerful revelation of both my strengths and weaknesses. Much to my delight, the entire class actively participated. Every first-grader in the class began singing and following along. What I discovered first was that I am really good at teaching, leading, and getting others engaged in the learning process. These are my strengths, or five-talent areas.

As our time of worship continued, I glanced over the classroom and noticed that some children had their hands cupped over their ears in an attempt to cover up our off-key musical mess. It was actually kind of cute. These children were doing their best to follow along; they just didn't like the noise we were making. The second thing I discovered that day is that I'm not a very good musician. I just don't have the talent needed to play an instrument and sing on key.

I spent the next few years attempting to improve my musical talent before eventually letting it go, and I am proud to say that I did eventually let this go. Music is something that I enjoyed doing and there would have been nothing wrong with sticking with it, but no matter how hard I worked, I would never have become a great musician. Because there are many other things I also enjoy, I made the conscious choice to pour my time and energy into areas where I have the God-given talent needed to excel.

Choosing to Build on Strengths

One of psychology's more recent discoveries is that people who perform well do so by building on their strengths. Natural ability combined with hard work produces dynamic results. When we discover and develop our God-given strengths, we thrive. Choice theory encourages us to focus on what we can do as opposed to becoming bitter about what we can't do. Like many singers on the television show *American Idol*, I could have spent years taking music and singing lessons only to develop into a mediocre singer at best. In fact, *American Idol* demonstrates the power of focusing on strengths. Singers who have natural talent gain experience, build on their strength and excel, while singers who have years of practice but lack natural ability are left behind. We put our strengths to work when we focus our time and energy on building on the momentum we already have.

You can begin discovering your strengths by answering the following questions:

- In what areas do I already excel?

- What do I enjoy doing? (Most of the time, operating in the area of our strengths also produces joy).
- In what areas do others tell me that I excel?

God has given you your specific strengths for a reason. There is no one else quite like you. While sometimes it will be necessary to build up weaknesses in order to prevent them from holding us back, exceling and thriving are direct results of focusing on our strengths.

2. Make wise choices daily.

Small choices made over time generate momentum and magnify results. The well-known fable of the tortoise and the hare is an excellent reminder of the value of consistency. If you're not familiar with this tale, it's about a slow and steady tortoise and a very quick hare who decide to race. While this fable has been told in a variety of ways over the years, the hare always gets off to a quick start, leaving the tortoise in a cloud of dust. After gaining a strong lead, the hare tires out. Seeing that he is so far ahead and spying a comfortable patch of grass under a shady tree, the hare feels confident enough to stop for a quick break. Unfortunately for the hare, he ends up dozing off, and the tortoise passes him while he is asleep. The tortoise's slow and steady pace allows him to win the race. In the classic cartoon version, the hare wakes up from his nap due to the cheers of the crowd watching the tortoise approach the finish line. The hare runs at top speed, gaining ground, but it's not enough. The tortoise wins in a dramatic photo finish.

No matter how many times this story is told and in how many different ways, the tortoise wins the race every time. Sometimes I feel like the tortoise. When it comes to talents, I feel like others have the flashy and fancy gifts that get them ahead in life. Yet it's not those who get off to a strong start but those who finish the race who win in the end. The wise choices we make may initially appear small and insignificant, but they accumulate over time to produce massive results. Like the tortoise, slow and steady wins the race.

Small, positive choices made on a daily basis help us to build momentum, and momentum is a powerful ally. A steam engine provides an excellent example of the power of positive momentum at work. When a steam engine is still, it can easily be held in place by a small, slanted block placed under the front tire. Yet a train moving at full force will press though most any obstacle in its path. Similarly, when we have little positive momentum in our lives, we work hard and feel like we are getting nowhere. Accomplishing anything takes an enormous amount of effort. It may feel like we are swimming through syrup, putting out tons of energy and getting nowhere fast. On the other hand, when we have momentum on our side, we visibly see and experience the payoff of our efforts. A 1960s experiment involving children and marshmallows powerfully illustrates how small, wise choices accumulate over time to produce powerful results.

Marshmallow Wisdom

In the 1960s and 1970s, Walter Mischel led a team of researchers in conducting what is now known as the famous Stanford Marshmallow Experiment. In this study, a child was placed alone in a room with a small treat which, no surprise here, was most often a marshmallow, although sometimes cookies and pretzels were used as well. The child was told that he could eat the treat immediately if he wanted to, but   if he waited for the host to return he would receive two treats. The presenter would then leave the room for about 15 minutes, leaving the child alone with the coveted marshmallow.

This experiment was repeated multiple times with different children. Some children wasted no time, instantly scarfing down the marshmallow. Others attempted to hold out by trying to distract themselves before eventually giving into temptation. A few were able to wait the entire 15 minutes. Though the decision not to eat a single marshmallow may seem like a small, insignificant choice, the study produced remarkable results. In the years that followed, the researchers continued to monitor these same children, tracking their ups and downs in life. It was discovered that the children who did not eat the marshmallow grew up to have higher Scholastic Aptitude Test (SAT) scores, a lower body mass index (meaning they were physically healthier), and higher education achievements than their peers who had eaten the marshmallow. The self-discipline they demonstrated in a small area of life had snowballed and resulted in success in a multitude of areas.

Proverbs 28:20 states, "A faithful person will have an abundance of blessings." Faithfulness in the little things adds up over time to produce big results.

3. Give up attempts at changing others.

As mentioned, in choice theory, attempts to force others to do what they don't want to do are known as external control psychology. William Glasser believed that the causes of many human miseries stem from the use of external control psychology. From my work with families, it's hard to disagree with him. I've come in contact with countless individuals who took an active role in creating a very chaotic and miserable situation for themselves and those around them by trying to control the actions of others. One of the problems with external control psychology is that it adds increased pressure to an already intense situation. It says, "This concern must be addressed and resolved now!" as opposed to allowing others the opportunity to grow, develop, and change over time.

The destructiveness of external control psychology is seen in the story of Naboth and King Ahaz found in 1 Kings, Chapter 21. In this historical narrative, King Ahaz, the king of Israel, gazes out of his palace window and notices a flourishing vineyard nearby. The location was perfect, the vineyard beautiful, and the fruit looked delicious. In that instant, Ahaz set his heart on buying this field. He made the owner, a man by the name of Naboth, a fair offer, but received in reply a report that the land was an inheritance passed down from generation to generation. Naboth was not willing to sell for any price. Upon hearing this, the king was devastated. He flung himself on his bed in a fit of despair. When his wife, Jezabel, found her husband having an adult-size temper tantrum in his bedroom, she devised a plan to have Naboth killed so the king could take possession of the vineyard he so greatly desired.

Jezabel immediately set her evil plot into action. She hired two false witnesses to report they heard Naboth curse God and the king, a crime that carried the penalty of death. Her plan worked flawlessly. At the report of the two lying witnesses, Naboth was executed, allowing the king the freedom to take ownership of the vineyard. Although the plan succeeded, God was not pleased. He sent the prophet Elijah to confront King Ahaz, which set off a series of events leading to Jezabel's death and ongoing trouble for the king.

This is a dark story where no one goes on to live happily ever after. Rarely does the use of external control psychology produce positive results. The more insistent we become in our demands of others, the more damaging the outcome will be.

Giving up external control psychology tools can be difficult to do, and it can be especially challenging for parents. Before giving up these strategies entirely, it's important to know that the Bible does make a case for using some external control psychology tools in certain situations. For example, the following verses present a case for using these types of tools:

- *Proverbs 22:6* "Train a child in the way that he should go, and when he is old he will not turn from it."
- *Proverbs 13:24* "The one who spares his rod hates his child, but the one who loves his child is diligent in disciplining him."

Child training, as mentioned in Proverbs 22:6, involves the use of rewards and consequences, which are a mild to moderate form of coercion, and Proverbs 13:24 presents a case for the use of stronger discipline at times. Completely eliminating all forms of external control psychology may be impractical, especially in regard to parenting a strong-willed child. But creative parents will look for opportunities to limit its use.

What I have noticed in my work with families is that often, external control psychology is the first step taken, when it would better serve as a last resort. When external control psychology is implemented, it's best done intentionally, in small doses and only after choice theory techniques have been tried first. For example, one mother of three teenagers I know assigns each of these young adults a household chore. If they choose not to complete their chore, they have the option of paying another person in the home out of their own allowance to do it for them. There is no lecturing, yelling, or attempts at coercion. All the chores in the home get completed and the teens learn a valuable life lesson about the connection between work and money in the process.

External Control Psychology and Choice Theory Differences

External Control Psychology	Choice Theory
Focuses on changing the other person through rewards, punishments, manipulation, abuse, etc.	Focuses on the things that we can change.
Demands change now.	Accepts the other person where they are, and sets boundaries to limit the impact of negative behaviors.

Views others as being in control of our happiness and success.	Views happiness and success as a result of the choices we make.
Feels powerless and operates out of fear.	Feels powerful and operates out of hope, creativity, and love.
Sees one option (changing the other person).	Examines the many different options available and makes the best choice.
Gives consequences.	Allows natural consequences to take their course.

To identify the use of external control psychology, you can ask the following questions:

- Have I been attempting to control the actions of others through manipulation, rewards, strong persuasion, or force?
- Have I convinced myself that my happiness and success is based on the actions of others instead of the choices that I am able to make?
- Am I blaming others for things that I have the ability to change?

If you've answered yes to any of these questions, then now is a good time to begin replacing the thinking of external control psychology with the principles of choice theory.

You can do that by asking:

- What actions can I take to change this situation?
- What part did I play in creating this situation and what abilities do I have to change it?
- What is one specific action (even if it is a little step) that I can take right now to move things in the right direction?
- Do I need to begin separating myself from this person by setting boundaries in place that reduce the harm caused to me?

Setting up boundaries by limiting contact with those who consistently hurt us is a positive tool that can be used to replace demanding that the other person change. Boundaries are more effective than demands because demands don't have the ability to enforce change. On the other hand, boundaries are something we set and we enforce. Sometimes boundaries are imposed by limiting contact with the person who is causing us harm in order to prevent additional harm from occurring. Boundaries work because choosing how much time we spend with another person is something that is under our control. As you can see, we often have more power than we realize.

Families and close relationships are systems that connect and influence each other. Any change in one part of the system will result in changes in the other parts. Just as a pebble tossed into a pond creates ripples that extend to the shore, our actions influence the actions of those around us. The best way to change the actions of others is to begin with ourselves.

4. Focus on the Choices Available

The fourth principle is to focus on the positive choices we can make. God doesn't make any junk. The talents and abilities you have been given are exactly the ones you are supposed to have. God has given them to you for a reason. Choice theory teaches us that we have the ability to live a life of contentment and success by focusing on the things that we can do. However, using the principles of choice theory is not always easy and often requires creativity and a willingness to take risks.

Ken Ilgunas provides an excellent example of this. He embarked on an adventure of putting choice theory principles into action and is now reaping the benefits. His story happened like this: Ken graduated from the University of Buffalo in 2005 with a degree in English and History. Unfortunately, he completed his degree in the midst of a downed economy, and like many at that time, was unable to find a job in his chosen field.

His inability to begin his career was not due to a lack of effort on his part. Ken was turned down for 25 internships and, to make matters worse, had amassed a student loan debt of $32,000. At this point, Ken could have easily found reasons to become bitter and to blame others for his problems. It would have been easy to point the finger at the university, blaming them for not warning him that a degree in History and English was one of the least marketable areas of study. He could have blamed the internships for not choosing to take him on, or like many were doing at that time, blamed the downed economy. But instead of doing any of these things, Ken took charge of the situation.

For him, this meant packing up the few belongings he owned and moving to Alaska. This was where he was able to find a job that paid $9 an hour in addition to providing him with room and board. Ken soon found himself living miles from the nearest store and disconnected from cellphone service. But with these challenges also came opportunity. Decreased engagement with the outside world allowed Ken to save almost every dollar he earned and as a result, he was able to pay off his student loans entirely in just two short years. Ken then returned to Duke University to attend graduate school. This time, instead of taking on additional debt, he decided to live out of his van. Ken bought a 1994 Ford Econoline on Craigslist for $1,500 that also became his new home.

He spent the next few years attending graduate school where, due to his small living quarters, he spent the majority of his time in class, studying in the library, or at work. Ken put his creativity to the test. He charged all his electronic devices in the library and tutored children at a local elementary school to earn extra money for textbooks and classes. He also used his free time to write.

During this time he wrote a book about his adventures entitled *Walden on Wheels: On the Open Road from Debt to Freedom.*[4] As a result of his hard work, consistency, and creativity, Ken graduated in 2011 completely debt-free.

Ken Ilgunas is an excellent example of someone who chose to use the talents he was given. He discovered he did not like the situation he was in and implemented his God-given creativity to alter his circumstances, and head toward adventure and success.

5. Keep Moving Forward.

A fifth way of putting choice theory into practice is to keep moving forward with positive choices regardless of the actions of others. This principle is especially important because it is easy to succumb to peer pressure and follow others off-course. Choice theory encourages us to focus on the choices we can make and to continue making those choices regardless of the direction others choose to take. It involves following the advice of my grade-school teacher by focusing on what we are doing as opposed to focusing on those around us. Doing this is sometimes uncomfortable because it can mean going against the flow. But this can be a good thing.

An example of this type of wisdom is seen in the Biblical story of Joshua. Joshua is an outstanding example of a man who chose to hold firm to his values regardless of the decisions of others. He was a military general, the successor of Moses and the leader of the Nation of Israel. He was appointed by God to lead the Israelites into the land that God had promised to give to them. After accomplishing this colossal mission, Joshua divided up the land among the tribes of Israel. Then, before allowing everyone to return home, he made one final speech where he encouraged everyone to remain true to God. In this speech, Joshua spoke these words: "Choose today whom you will worship, whether it be the gods whom your ancestors worshiped beyond the Euphrates, or the gods of the Amorites in whose land you are living. But I and my family will worship the Lord!"[5]

This is choice theory at its best. Joshua didn't create unnecessary pressure by insisting, demanding, or coercing. Instead, he led by example. Joshua made his stance clear and allowed others the freedom to choose their own direction.

Choice theory seeks out the next right thing to do and does it regardless of what others may think. Sometimes this will involve going against what the popular thinking of the day says should be done. In a time where the cultural norm was to fashion images of many different gods, serving one invisible God was seen as weird. Yet it was also the right thing to do. To practice choice theory is to make calculated, wise choices. It involves creatively making use of all available resources. Choice theory reminds us that, no matter where we are currently in life, we have some power to change our situation by focusing on the things that we can do.

Life Lessons from Choice Theory

We have the freedom to improve our life and to positively influence others around us by altering the choices we make. We can choose to:

- *Discover our strengths and put them to work.*
- *Make wise choices daily.*
- *Give up attempts to control others.*
- *Focus on the choices we can make.*
- *Move forward in taking positive action regardless of the decisions of others.*

Questions for Additional Reflection and Discussion

1. Can you identify some specific times in your life where making small, wise choices on a consistent basis snowballed to have an enormous, positive effect?

2. Choice theory says we are where we are at in life because of our choices, and if we don't like where we are, we have the power to change our situation by altering the choices we make. Do you agree, partially agree, or disagree with this statement and why?

3. Are there any specific areas in your life where you need to change the choices you are making in order to arrive at a better outcome? What would making these changes look like?

4. Can you identify a time when someone attempted to use principles of external control psychology on you by attempting to coerce you into doing something you did not want to do? What was the end result of this and how did it impact your relationship with this person?

5. Can you identify a time where you attempted to use principles of external control psychology on someone else? What was the end result of this and how did it impact your relationship with this person?

6. Are there any areas in your life where you currently need to give up external control psychology principles and replace them with principles from choice theory? What would replacing these principles look like in your specific situation?

7. In this chapter, we examined a number of tools from choice theory including:

    - Discovering our strengths and putting them to work.
    - Making wise choices daily.
    - Giving up attempts to control others.
    - Focusing on the choices we can make.
    - Moving forward in taking positive action regardless of the decisions of others.

    Which one of these tools is most meaningful to you currently and what specific steps will you take or are you already taking to grow in this area?

Five

Connecting with Others:

Life Lessons from Attachment Theory

The more that we can give young people
opportunities to... observe firsthand how
sensitive, caring parents treat their offspring, the
more likely they are to follow suit.

~ John Bowlby

Point your kids in the right direction —
when they're old they won't be lost

~ Proverbs 22:6, *The Message*

Our childhood relationships matter and play a part in forming who we are. Yet, it's what we decide to do with these experiences as adults that completes our identity.

All of us, from the cradle to the grave, are happiest when life is organized as a series of excursions, long or short, from the secure base provided by our attachment figures."[1] These words were written by psychologist John Bowlby, a pioneer in the field of attachment, who brought attention to humanity's pressing need for close connections with others from the moment of conception. John's fascination with how children bond and fail to bond with their primary caregivers was fueled by his own childhood experiences, as well as two key historical events that brought attachment problems into public awareness.

John was born on February 26, 1907 to an upper-middle class family in London, England. As the fourth in a family of six children, John found himself in immediate competition for his parents' attention. Making things increasingly difficult was the fact that he grew up in an era when children were expected to be seen but not heard.

Throughout the school year, John was only permitted to see his mother for one hour each day. This brief period of bonding took place during tea time, with some additional time allotted during summer breaks. While this may sound unusual, it was the social norm of the day. The popular belief was that if parents spent too much time with their children and provided them with too much affection, it would lead to raising spoiled children.

Because of these beliefs, the amount of time John spent with his biological parents was intentionally limited, and he was raised primarily by his nanny, whom he would later describe as being the primary mother-figure in his life. Unfortunately, this mother-figure left the home when John was only four years old, resulting in his first major disruption in attachment. Then, at the age of seven, John was sent away to a boarding school. This was a second traumatic event that John would later write about in his book *Separation: Anxiety and Anger*, stating, "I wouldn't send a dog away to boarding school at age seven."

As a young adult, Bowlby studied psychology at Trinity College in Cambridge, and began his career by working with delinquent children. During World War II, Bowlby's fascination with attachment grew after witnessing two historic events that created an abrupt separation of many children from their parents and resulted in these families becoming inundated with attachment-related challenges. The two events included the evacuation of children from London in order to keep them safe from air raids and the creation of nurseries for infants in order to allow their parents to spend additional time contributing to the war effort.

As a side note, it's interesting to reflect on just how traumatic these events were to those who experienced them. The classic books, *The Secret Garden* and *The Lion, the Witch and the Wardrobe* are both about children whose adventures began when they were separated from their families as a result of these wartime evacuations. Last summer I read each of these books to my four and six-year-old daughters. When we reached the part in the stories that involved the children being sent away from their parents, both girls repeatedly asked, "Daddy, why did the children have to leave? Why, Daddy? But why?" No answer I gave was sufficient. My two girls instantly recognized these separations as unnatural and concerning.

These disruption events piqued the curiosity of John Bowlby, who wondered what types of long-term effects they would have on the children. These historic events, along with Bowlby's personal attachment and separation experiences, became the driving force leading to the formation of attachment theory. Next came Mary Ainsworth, a psychologist who further built upon the work of John Bowlby. Mary began her career as an assistant for Bowlby and took insights into attachments to the next level with the creation of the Strange Situation.

Experiments in Attachment

The Strange Situation was a series of experiments in attachment designed by Mary Ainsworth and her team of researchers. These experiments began in 1965 with the goal of gathering information regarding how young children use their bond with their mother to manage stress.

The experiments took place in a small room that resembled a waiting room in a doctor's office. The room contained a number of chairs, a variety of age-appropriate toddler toys, and a window made of one-way glass where May and her team could observe unnoticed. Approximately 100 middle class, American families participated in this study, and the children who participated were between the ages of twelve and eighteen months old. The "strange situation" scenario was conducted as follows: the mom would sit quietly in a chair and allow her child to play with the nearby toys. After a few minutes a stranger would enter the room, speak to the mother, and the mother would leave the room. The stranger, however, would stay. The absence of mom and the presence of the stranger created a strange situation upsetting the child.

After a brief period of time, the mom would re-enter the room and the stranger would leave. During the reuniting of mother and child, researchers paid careful attention to the various ways the children would use their bond with their mother to comfort themselves. Once the child had calmed down, the strange situation would be repeated in a slightly different manner.

This time, mom would exit the room first, and then the stranger would enter. This created a second strange situation that would again visibly upset the child. The experiment concluded with the mother returning to the room, the stranger leaving and the child with mom to find comfort. All of this coming and going provided researchers with the opportunity to observe attachment patterns. The entire experiment took about twenty minutes to complete and resulted in the discovery of four distinct patterns of behavior that have come to be known as attachment styles. Attachment styles describe how we emotionally connect to other important people in our lives. The four attachment styles include the avoidant attachment, ambivalent attachment, disorganized attachment and secure attachment.

Let's look at some of the key elements of each of these relational patterns first as they were evidenced in the Strange Situation experiment, then as they appear in the

Bible, and finally as they manifest in adulthood. As children, attachment styles reveal themselves in the following ways:

Avoidant Attachment Pattern

In the avoidant attachment, the toddler would ignore mom upon her return to the room. The distressed child would not acknowledge their mother's return with eye contact or bodily movement, but would sit fixated in distress. Avoidant children often ignore their attachments to significant others during periods of emotional self-regulation.

Ambivalent Attachment Pattern

The children with an ambivalent attachment were very suspicious of the stranger. They would quickly become upset when their mother left the room and would run to their mother upon her return. However, these children were not easily comforted by their mom. Instead, ambivalent children would communicate their anxiety by becoming overly clingy and dependent. Ambivalence is characterized by having mixed feelings and emotions. It says, "On one hand I love you and need you and on the other hand I'm very upset with you and want you to know it." Other children demonstrated their ambivalence by acts of physical aggression such as hitting or pushing their mom upon her return. Ambivalent children anxiously cling to their attachment figures or lash out in anger during periods of emotional self-regulation.

Disorganized Attachment Pattern

Disorganized children would appear confused upon their mother's return. Their behaviors often included freezing and rocking. These children might attempt to approach mom with their backs turned toward her, or would begin running to her, only to freeze up, sit down, and ignore her a moment later. Disorganized children were described by observers as disoriented and confused. Today we know that this type of behavior pattern is frequently associated with a history of abuse and neglect. The disorganized child vacillates between extremes in avoidance and ambivalence.

Secure Attachment Pattern

Children with a secure attachment would become upset when their mother left the room. Upon her return, secure children would run to their mothers to find comfort. They would then feel safe enough to venture out on their own and begin playing or exploring the room. This attachment style is seen as the model of healthy attachment. Secure children use their mother as a safe haven for comfort without becoming overly clingy or avoidant. Mom becomes a secure base where they can fill up with the care needed before venturing out to explore the world.

As research into attachments progressed, it was recognized that similar patterns of attachment are present in adults. Our attachment styles begin forming in childhood and they never go away. This leads us to one of the greatest life lessons from attachment theory. In order to thrive, everyone needs healthy, secure attachments in their life. What is interesting is that not only are each of these four attachment styles found in adults, they are also present in the Bible. Learning to recognize the signs of each attachment style is important because it allows us to identify positive and negative attachment patterns in our own life and work to improve them. When we recognize insecure patterns of attachment, we can intentionally make adjustments toward a more secure style of relating.

Before looking at the different attachment styles as they appear in the Scriptures, let's take a minute to examine some important facts about adult attachment:

- Attachment styles describe us, but don't define us. They are not a diagnosis or pathology. They do describe a pattern of how we most often relate to significant people in our lives.

- Everyone will have one primary attachment style and will also display bits and pieces from each of the other three styles. It's okay if you see yourself in more than one attachment style—most people do.

- People often attach differently in their various relationships. You might discover that in some relationships you lean toward a secure attachment, while in others, you show signs of being anxious, avoidant, or disorganized. The goal is to learn to connect to others in a secure way. Learning to attach securely to others is a process, not an event. Heading down this path might mean first discovering how to attach securely in those relationships that are the safest with the goal of transitioning to a more secure style in other relationships in the future.

- The goal of learning about attachment styles is to become more secure in our own relationships. No one is completely secure in all of their relationships. The good news is that we can grow in the way that we relate to others and if you come to realize that you relate primarily to the avoidant, ambivalent, or disorganized attachment style, you can make the choice to begin connecting to others in a more secure way right now. Positive growth is possible and encouraged!

- The closer we move to a pattern of secure attachment, the healthier and less chaotic our relationships will be.

How we relate matters. The importance of positive connection to others is a theme that runs throughout Scripture. As we examine the four attachment styles, you will want to take mental notes of which style most frequently depicts you and how this relational pattern influences the quality of your connections to others.

Adam, Eve, and the Avoidant Attachment

In the Bible, attachment styles are present from the beginning of Genesis. Adam and Eve, the first man and woman who ever lived, provide a clear example of the avoidant attachment style. Their story is found in Genesis chapter three, and begins after God's creation of the heavens and earth. On the sixth day of creation, God formed Adam from the dust of the ground and a short time later fashioned Eve out of one of Adam's ribs. God put Adam in charge of tending the Garden of Eden, and life is good. God tells Adam that he is free to eat fruit from any tree in the Garden except for one. Adam is told to avoid the tree in the middle of the Garden, called the Tree of the Knowledge of Good and Evil, and warned that to eat from this tree would result in death.

However, a short time later, Satan came to Eve in the form of a serpent, tempting her to taste of the forbidden fruit. Eve is deceived and she eats. She also gives some to her husband and he disobeys as well. After these acts of defiance, the avoidant attachment style makes its appearance. Adam and Eve hide from God. God calls for Adam, and when confronted, Adam attempts to evade. He begins by pointing his finger at Eve (which must have put a very rocky start to the first marriage). Adam states that the events leading up to the consumption of the fruit occurred because of "…the woman you (God) gave me."[2] Not only does Adam shrink back from his responsibility, but in one breath he manages to both blame his wife and hint that God might have some responsibility in the matter! Following Adam's lead, Eve points her finger at the serpent, taking another go at evading accountability.

Like Adam and Eve, those with an avoidant attachment style shiver at the thought of conflict. For the avoidant, hiding and blaming others is more comfortable than tackling the challenge directly. When this attachment style is implemented, strong relationship bonds are loosened slowly and silently. Minor conflicts fester over time. When confronted, the avoidant may attempt to hide or might attempt to shift the blame onto someone else. The avoidant will do just about anything to evade conflict. Adults with an avoidant attachment style may:

- Be emotionally over-regulated by displaying controlled emotional highs and lows.
- Have a limited emotional vocabulary. They are more likely to use the words "I think..." than "I feel... "
- Be prone to addictions as way of self-medicating and drowning out feelings.
- Feel an inner loneliness inside while presenting as self-reliant and calm on the outside.
- When confronted, may distance themselves, withdraw, or become defensive.
- Seem innocent of wrong-doing due to their tendency to hide under the radar.
- May be hyper-responsible in an attempt to avoid stirring up conflict.
- Have problems with intimacy. I once heard intimacy pronounced "in-to-me-see," which is the ability to allow others to peer into our inner-world. It involves letting others "see" what is going on inside of our hearts and souls.

Martha and the Ambivalent Attachment

The story of Mary and Martha is found in Luke 10:38-42 and provides a prime example of the ambivalent attachment style at work. These two sisters were close friends of Jesus and had offered to open their home to

Jesus and His disciples whenever they needed a place to rest. One day, Jesus and the disciples stopped by unexpectedly. The women were honored to have Jesus in their home, and each reacted very differently. With the arrival of Jesus, a crowd gathered, and Jesus began to teach. Mary chose to join the crowd, relaxing, sitting at Jesus' feet and soaking in what He had to say. Martha, on the other hand, felt anxiety surging within. Her mind flooded with thoughts of the preparations that needed to be done. There were floors to clean, meals to cook, and hundreds of minor details to attend to. This attention to detail is what made Martha an exceptional hostess. It also had the tendency to become a cruel taskmaster that did not allow her to relax... ever.

As Martha began forming her mental checklist, her anxiety continued to build, and as she attended to the tasks at hand she found herself becoming increasingly frustrated. The tension continued to swell within her until finally, in a fit of exasperation, Martha blurted out, "Lord, don't you care that my sister has left me to do all the work alone? Tell her to help me." Jesus answered softly, "Martha, Martha, you are worried and troubled about many things, but one thing is needed. Mary has chosen the best part; it will not be taken away from her."[3]

Like Martha, those with an ambivalent attachment style are anxious about many things. They have a hard time relaxing and letting go. Often, there is the underlying belief that one must do something to get his or her needs met. Ambivalents have a performance-based view of love, and fear that if they don't measure up, love will be withdrawn. Unable to feel affirmed on their own, ambivalents look to others as their source of validation. Because of this, abandonment and rejection are feared the most.

The underlying belief of the ambivalent is that others around them are capable while they are not. Feeling helpless, the ambivalent may become clingy and over-dependent. If they still don't get their needs met, these feelings of uneasiness may reveal themselves through a childish outburst of anger made in an attempt to get others to do for them what they feel incapable of doing themselves. Adults who lean toward the ambivalent attachment style:

- Have a damaged sense of identity that results in inner anxiety.
- May become emotionally dependent on others.
- Have emotions that are under-regulated, resulting in explosive outbursts, blaming, and pursuing when upset. (This is a person who will follow you when he or she is in distress, insisting that the issue be resolved now.)
- Because they are so in tune with their feelings, they can be empathetic and charming on some occasions, and clingy and needy at other times.
- They will often appear to "be the problem" due to their emotionality and reactivity.

- May have difficulty being alone due to their need of others.
- Are emotionally expressive and use words like, "I feel..."
- Tend to base their decisions more on emotions than on reason and logic.

King Saul and the Disorganized Attachment

The relationship between King Saul and his son-in-law, David, demonstrates many characteristics of the disorganized attachment style. As Saul's story illustrates, this attachment style is characterized by chaos and unpredictability. It is sometimes, though not always, connected to severe pathology. Being connected to someone with a disorganized attachment style can be emotionally exhausting. Saul's story is told throughout the book of 1 Samuel. Some of the highlights that demonstrate the disorganized attachment style are as follows:

Saul was anointed king by the prophet Samuel and became the first king over the nation of Israel. His initial contact with David comes as a result of being tormented by an evil spirit. Seeing Saul's anguish, his advisers suggested that a skilled musician be brought in to play for Saul whenever he becomes distressed, and David, a young shepherd and capable musician, is enlisted to play the harp in Saul's presence.

Fast-forward a few years. Saul is rejected by God as king due to an act of disobedience. He is aware that God has rejected him and that his time as king is limited. Saul's popularity among the people is also beginning to dwindle. King Saul begins to feel threatened and enters into a chaotic and confusing connection with David. Eventually, the only thing that David knows for certain is that when it comes to King Saul, absolutely anything can happen next.

After David's well-known victory over the giant, Goliath, King Saul appoints David as a high-ranking officer in his army. Initially their relationship heads in a positive direction, and David continues to play music for the king when he becomes distressed. However, one day, instead of being soothed by the music, King Saul becomes increasingly upset and attempts to murder David by attempting to pin him to the wall with his spear. David evades the king's two unsuccessful attempts to take his life. Then, shortly after this incident, King Saul vacillates to the opposite extreme by offering David the hand of his oldest daughter, Merab, in marriage. David politely declines, stating that he is not worthy to be a part of the king's family. After repeated attempts, Saul eventually succeeds in convincing David to marry his younger daughter, Michal.

However, after David agrees, Saul uses the approaching marriage as an opportunity to try to quietly remove David from the picture. The king asks David for 100 Philistine foreskins as dowry for the marriage while secretly hoping that David does not survive the collection process. But David does succeed. This success fuels David's ever-growing fame and intensifies the king's insecurity. David marries Michal, and following the marriage, Saul makes yet another attempt on David's life. This time, David flees the city. He is pursued by Saul, and during the chase, David gains the upper hand. In an odd twist, David and his men hide in a cave. Saul has to relieve himself and happens to choose the same cave David and his men are hiding in to do his business. Although the king is vulnerable, David refuses to take advantage of the situation, stating that he will not strike down God's anointed king.

After Saul exits the cave, David and his men make their presence known. King Saul is aware that David could have easily taken his life and elected not to. The king speaks to David from a distance, calling David "my son" and affirming the fact that one day David will rule as king. Saul returns home and stops pursuing David for a time, only to pick up the pursuit a short while later. And back and forth the story goes. The king continues to vacillate between honoring David and attempting to eliminate him. The relationship between the two is disorganized, confusing, and chaotic.

While this is an extreme example of the disorganized attachment style, it demonstrates the unpredictability and relational chaos that can result. Saul is charming and generous one moment only to transform into being harsh and vindictive the next. Those connected to friends and family with a disorganized style of attachment never know what to expect. Those with a disorganized adult attachment style may:

- Experience inner confusion and turmoil.
- Not know how to approach others to get their needs met.
- Experience inner emotional storms consisting of intense feelings of despair and helplessness.
- Vacillate between extremes by going from one extreme to another (i.e. "I love you..." becomes "I hate you..." or, "You're my best friend..." changes to "I want nothing to do with you...").
- Display characteristics of both the avoidant and ambivalent attachment styles, alternating between the two.
- Often have chaotic childhood experiences.

Jesus and the Secure Attachment Style

While there are numerous Biblical examples of the secure attachment style, Jesus sets the ultimate example of what it means to connect to others in a secure manner. Throughout His earthly ministry, Jesus modeled self-assurance, courage and a full range of emotions. He wept at the death of His dear friend Lazarus,[4] and confidently approached the disciples with the request that they leave their jobs behind to follow Him.[5] He boldly rebuked Peter,[6] and in a burst of frustration, overturned the Temple tables of the money changers, cleansing the courtyard of those who were attempting to make God's holy sanctuary into a place of business and merchandise.[7] When approached by His mother at a wedding, Jesus initially refused her request to help. He later changed His mind and performed His first public miracle of turning water into wine.[8] In the Garden of Gethsemane Jesus prayed, asking God to spare him from the crucifixion, yet ended His prayer affirming his desire for God's will to be done, even if it meant going against His own will.[8]

Jesus was able to fully express his emotions in appropriate ways. He was secure enough to say "no" and confident enough to know that it's acceptable to change one's mind. Jesus was bold, strong, and firm at times, while compassionate and gentle at others. Someone who is secure in their attachments is able to:

- Give and receive love without shame, guilt, or fear.
- Feel safe living in the world. He or she is able to look back and laugh at mistakes. This type of person can accept his own flaws as well the flaws of others.
- Enjoy spending time with others and enjoy time alone.
- Express a full range of emotions in a balanced and appropriate way. They are composed enough to

express both positive and negative emotions including feelings of joy, sadness, anger, and frustration.

- Is confident enough to know that it's okay for them to make one decision and later change their mind.
- Empathize with the feelings of others.
- Make his or her needs known. This person can ask for what they want and is also able to accept the situation when told "no" without becoming devastated.
- Is self-assured enough to set limits on harmful relationships and is able to stay away from abusive situations.

Life Lessons from Attachment Theory

Studies show that those who possess traits of a secure attachment style are better adjusted, have less anxiety, and have higher overall feelings of wellbeing, when compared to those who do not connect securely to others. Attachment theory teaches us, first and foremost, that relationships are important. Because of this, it is imperative that we give top priority to our interactions with others.

God designed us to connect. We see this in the first chapters of Genesis, where after creating the first man, God proclaimed "it is not good for man to be alone."[10]

Because of this, God created woman. What stands out in this passage is that God saw the need for Adam to connect to other human beings in spite of the fact that God Himself would walk with him at the end of each day. Although God had a face-to-face relationship with Adam, He still acknowledged Adam's need for face-to-face relationships with other human beings. Like Adam, you and I are born with a need to connect with others, and modern-day research confirms this.

Carefully designed studies have examined the impact of God as a positive attachment figure in people's lives. One such study examined the impact of God as a compensatory attachment figure. In other words, this study sought to discover if a relationship with God could take the place of a relationship with other human beings. The results brought to light that, although an attachment to God is vital, those who attempt to attach securely to God as a way of compensating for previous, poor social relationships will experience increased anxiety and overall decreased feelings of wellbeing when compared to those with secure attachments to other human beings.

The study also found that those who attempted to use God alone as a way of healing relational insecurities eventually carried over their anxious and insecure attachment styles into their relationship with God.[11] Instead of the supernatural relationship being a means of working through attachment issues, these issues seeped into the divine connection. Attachment issues are created during our interactions with other human beings and must be worked though in interactions with other humans. Asking God for guidance in healing attachment wounds is an excellent first step. James 1:5 says, "But if anyone is deficient in wisdom, he should ask God, who gives to all generously and without reprimand, and it will be given to him." God will give us wisdom to work through attachment challenges but will not allow us to solve these issues apart from others.

Three Ways to Move toward Security

So how do we begin moving toward more secure attachments? In addition to asking God for wisdom, here are three additional ways to move toward security:

1. Follow Secure Examples

Take a minute to think of the most secure person you know. Try to get a strong mental image of the qualities this person possesses. See if you can picture how this person carries himself. Think about the words he uses, his tone of voice, his facial expressions, and his gestures. Then ask yourself, "What would this person do in my particular situation?" Do your best to not only answer the question but to visualize the answer. The goal is to create a crystal-clear movie in your mind of how this person would act and communicate if they were in your shoes. Now, see if there are bits and pieces of this visualized scenario that you can copy. Perhaps there are other parts that you could adjust to make them fit better with your style.

❧

The goal of this exercise is to "borrow" the secure attachment style of someone you know well. This is similar to the therapeutic technique known as modeling. In modeling, the therapist demonstrates a specific skill such as assertive communication, sharing feelings, or performing a confidant introduction to a stranger. You can think of the securely attached person you are picturing as your model for secure attachment. By visualizing how they handle themselves and then practicing those traits yourself, you will eventually integrate their secure attachment characteristics into your own life. The best way to develop a secure attachment style is to begin acting in a secure manner regardless of how you feel.

Doing this may feel awkward at first, and that's okay. Secure feelings follow secure actions. Although it may take time, secure feelings will eventually come. Visualizing a secure person, adopting their secure style, and acting in a secure manner despite feelings of apprehension are great first steps toward growing toward a more secure style of attachment.

2. Practice In-to-me-see Daily

Intimacy, or "in-to-me-see" involves allowing others to peer into our inner world. It means sharing our thoughts, feelings, and opinions with others, letting down our guard, taking off the masks we put on, and allowing those closest to us to connect with the real us… warts and all. Doing this is both exciting and scary. It's exciting because it opens up the opportunity to be understood, accepted, and loved for who we really are. It can be scary because it involves becoming vulnerable and opens up the risk of rejection. Because of this, intimacy is something that should be reserved for the safe people in our lives.

Intimacy does not need to be practiced with everyone. In fact, in the *DSM* there is a disorder that describes indiscriminate attachment to others. It is called Reactive Attachment Disorder. This disorder is divided into two types: the inhibited type and the disinhibited type. The first avoids close connections to others while the second indiscriminately attempts to connect to everyone at a deep emotional level. Both extremes are unhealthy. Healthy intimacy is developed through a process of connecting with safe people over time. Trust grows as each person in the relationship reveals more of their inner world.

A relationship with intimacy seeks to create an atmosphere where mistakes are okay. It is a place where we are valued for our strengths, weaknesses, and varying opinions. In casual relationships the motto may be, "I'm okay and you're okay." When we ask how someone is doing, the expected answer is "Fine" or "Great." Real, honest answers are frowned upon because they rock the boat. Intimate relationships are different. The motto is, "I'm not okay and you're not okay and that's okay." There is an unspoken agreement that perfection is not allowed. In close, safe relationships, if we try to act like we have everything together, our failure to be genuine will be called out in a spirit of compassion and grace. These types of relationships are important because they foster healing and allow us to be known and loved for who we are.

Teflon® is a smooth material used to coat cooking pans. Burn an egg on a Teflon® pan and it will slide right off. I love Teflon® in our kitchen. It has allowed our pots and pans to survive many of my most dreadful cooking catastrophes. Like a kitchen pan, some people have Teflon® exteriors. They are smooth and clean on the outside, refusing to expose their rough edges, hurts, and needs on the inside. Teflon® is an excellent coating on pans, but a terrible exterior for humans. Those who hide their flaws limit their ability to connect with others. Attempts at friendship slide right off. It is our rough edges, our failures, our needs, and our desires that make us human. These rough edges provide a connection point that allows friendships to stick.

People connect best to other human beings and humans are by nature imperfect. Romans 3:23 says, "All have sinned and fall short of the glory of God." God knows we are imperfect, and deep down, so does everyone else. Honest connections with others not only create intimacy in the relationships, but also provide an atmosphere where growth can take place.

Proverbs 27:17 says, "As iron sharpens iron, so one person sharpens another." But sharpening is impossible without disclosure. When we share our struggles with others, we have the opportunity to glean wisdom from their experiences. As you can see, intimacy is important because it leads to deeper levels of connection and growth.

3. Identify Insecurities, Make Amends and Move Forward

The third step in moving toward a secure attachment involves learning to accept the imperfections in our lives and finding ways to manage them well. No one is completely secure all of the time and this is okay. Acting insecurely at times is less than ideal, but it's also part of what it means to be human.

When we recognize that we are acting in an ambivalent, avoidant, or disorganized way, it is an opportunity for us to do additional attachment work, furthering our growth. Philippians 1:6 says, "For I am sure of this very thing, that the one who began a good work in you will perfect it until the day of Christ Jesus." You and I are in an ongoing process of growth that will not be complete until that wonderful day when Christ returns. Until then, we will have failures and shortcomings. We can attempt to ignore them, we can try to hide them from others, or we can use them as a catalyst for growth.

In Matthew 18:15, Jesus provides a model for secure attachment when He states, "If your brother sins, go and show him his fault when the two of you are alone. If he listens to you, you have regained your brother." When we are wronged, the secure thing to do is to confront the person gently and directly. When we are guilty of being the offender, after our wrongdoings are brought to our attention, the healthy thing to do is to admit our mistakes, make amends if possible, and then move on.

Acting imperfectly is part of being human and making amends when we are guilty of wrongdoing is a sign of security. Apologizing does not mean we are "bad" or "evil" although sometimes we may be guilty of doing bad things. Secure people are confident enough to know that they are not defined by a single action. Beating ourselves up over mistakes is not helpful. Through the work of Christ we have already been forgiven. Since God has forgiven us, we can let go of the matter too, leaving the past in the past and moving forward toward our bright future ahead.

As you can see, having close, secure attachments to others is important. God designed us to be in relationships. By paying attention to how we attach to others we add value to our life and to the lives of those around us. From the cradle to the grave, we thrive when we live securely connected to others.

Life Lessons from Attachment Theory

We are created to connect securely with others. We can foster this secure attachment style by:

- *Following the example of other secure people in our lives.*
- *Practicing intimacy by sharing our inner world with safe people.*
- *Recognizing insecurities, making amends when possible, and then moving forward.*

Questions for Additional Reflection and Discussion

1. Which attachment style do you find yourself relating to most often and how do the traits from this attachment style play out in your life?

2. Can you identify some times in your life when you have attached to others in an avoidant or ambivalent way? What was the outcome? What might have happened if you had used a more secure way of relating in this situation?

3. What traits from the secure attachment style are currently your strengths and what is one specific thing you could do this week to build on this strength?

4. What traits from the secure attachment style are more challenging for you? What is one specific thing you could do this week to grow in this area?

5. How does the idea of developing 'in-to-me-see' make you feel? Who are two or three safe people in your life who you could develop or continue developing this type of relationship with?

6. Do you need to grow in your secure attachment style by:

- Following the example of another secure person in your life?
- Practicing intimacy by sharing your inner world with someone close to you?
- Acknowledging past, insecure actions, making amends and moving on?

If so, what specific steps will you take to put this into practice this week?

Six

The Power of Being:

Life Lessons from Person-Centered Therapy

The curious paradox is that when I accept myself
just as I am, then I can change.

~ Carl Rogers

He (Jesus) didn't, and doesn't, wait for us to get
ready. He presented himself for this sacrificial
death when we were far too weak and rebellious
to do anything to get ourselves ready.

~ Romans 5:8 *The Message*

It's not the words we say, but how we make others feel when they're in our presence that causes relationships to last.

Relationships matter. You and I have an intense, God-designed longing to bond with other human beings — a need that can only be met within the context of compassionate, engaged, grace-filled relationships. These types of connections are the ones that influence us most. If you think back to the best teachers, mentors and coaches in your life, you'll likely find that it was who they were, rather than the specific actions they took, that mattered most.

Perhaps it was their warm personality, the way their face lit up when you entered the room. Or maybe it was their willingness to have an honest, no-holds-barred, "I'm going to tell you what you need to hear even if it hurts" conversation that helped get you get back on track. Or possibly it was their ability to share in your ups and downs without ever losing faith that in the end you would pull through.

If we had to boil down what all of the best mentors, teachers, coaches, pastors, therapists, mom and dads, aunts, uncles and cousins have in common, we could sum it up in the word "being." These people influenced us by:

- Being present
- Being caring
- Being tough and compassionate at exactly the same time
- Being open, honest and real
- Being grace-filled
- And most of all, by being themselves

It was who they were, combined with their willingness to share their lives with us, that made all the difference.

Present and Engaged

There is a phrase that is used for people who have lost the ability to fully participate in the here and now. It's called "going through the motions" and if you've ever worked with, talked to, or spent time in the presence of someone who does this, you know that it's not a lot of fun. The phrase itself is remarkably descriptive as it portrays that work is getting accomplished, but there is no passion behind what is being done. Hollow eyes and a distant, far-off gaze are accompanied by the phrase,

"Huh... Did you just say something?" Those who have lost their sense of being are also described as checked out, burned out and lost in thought. Unfortunately, this happens far too often, and when it does:

- Careers become about efficiency and carrying out the next task, with little enthusiasm for what is being accomplished.
- Teaching turns into a cold, mechanical relaying of information.
- Following Christ is reduced to a rigid set of rules and beliefs.
- Parenting is transformed from a warm bond to upholding a strict standard of "do's" and "don'ts."
- Therapy gets boiled down to a set of impersonal tools and techniques.
- And the daily routine is reduced to an exercise of checking one item after another off of our to-do list.

Fervor and excitement vanish as the person enters "task-mode." Everyone does this at times, and it's not all bad. There is a time and a place for getting work done, and truth be told, it's impossible to remain 100 percent zealous about everything we do — that would be exhausting. The concept of "being" isn't black and white. There is a broad spectrum to our levels of engagement and some activities require that we be more fully present than others.

What is unfortunate is when being partially checked in becomes a consistent pattern in relationships, resulting in half-hearted, just enough to get by, overly hurried, multi-tasking, stressed out, and listening with one ear types of interactions. One example of this is found in Matthew 15:8 which says, "This people honors me with their lips, but their heart is far from me." The proper actions were there, but they had little meaning because of the lack of fervor behind them.

Letting Go of the Good to Take Hold of the Great

In relationships, full engagement is imperative, but it isn't easy to give and certainly isn't getting any easier. Our world is filled with an overabundance of good things clamoring for our attention. Attending to relationships involves learning to let go of some of the good in order to take hold of something truly great — being fully present for the important people in our lives.

As a college professor, I can attest to both how difficult and vital this is. Teaching isn't easy, and instructors tend to fall into the bad habit of excessively focusing on the course material to the neglect of student engagement, resulting in important opportunities for life-changing impact being missed. But the best teachers not only educate, they also genuinely care about their students and live out what they teach. These instructors are fully present in the moment and are willing to sacrifice the good — such as covering every minute detail in the lesson plan — for the great, things like answering questions and taking advantage of the teachable moments that unexpectedly arise during class. As a result, these teachers not only impart information, but share a part of themselves as well.

Similarly, while good leaders know that completing tasks is necessary, the best leaders understand that it's their connection to other people that's most important. Skilled leaders are much more than accomplishers; they have the ability to connect their unique style to the work at hand and possess an excitement for the mission that is contagious.

Christ followers also understand the importance of full engagement and have popularized two phrases that emphasize this. The first says, "Christianity is not a religion, it's a relationship," and the second is the catchphrase, "More Jesus, less religion." Both statements accentuate the value of connection. Religion and relationships are like oil and water, toothpaste and orange juice, and submarines and screen doors: they don't mix well. Dictionary.com defines religion as, "a specific fundamental set of beliefs and practices generally agreed upon by a number of persons." Religion places its focus on a consistent pattern of doing. It says pray more, study more, do more good deeds, attend church habitually and parent in such and such a manner. The list of "shoulds" in religion is unending. There is always one more good thing on the list that needs to be done.

On the other hand, relationships accentuate shared moments together and provide the freedom to relax, breathe-easy and be ourselves. From a relational approach, connecting with God might involve attending church, or it could mean enjoying a good cup of coffee while watching the sunrise and meditating on God's greatness. There is no one specific outline that must be followed. The routine activities found in religion are fine if they draw us closer to our creator, but they are a cruel task-master when they become one more item that we feel obligated to check off our to-do list. While prayer, Bible study and regular church attendance are all good, wise believers understand that it's the close connection to God that is truly great, and in some cases, the good may need to be given up (or at least the routine pattern altered) in order for the great to transpire.

Moving from Good to Great in Relationships

In our most cherished relationships, the most significant value does not come in the "doing," but in the "being." This means the primary focus is neither on the activities nor the accomplishments, but rather on enjoying each other's presence. When my wife and I began dating, we had some exhilarating adventures together. Sunset hikes on the beach, parasailing in Catalina, stand-up paddle boarding at the bay and snorkeling with leopard sharks are all fond memories of our early excursions. Yet these dates were not really about these activities at all. While the events themselves were fun, it was being with my future wife that mattered most.

Entering into this state of attentiveness involves letting go of personal agendas and tuning in to the other person. Ecclesiastes 3 poetically describes how there is a time for everything, including "a time to keep silent, and a time to speak."[1] There are two noteworthy things about this passage of Scripture. The first is that there is an appropriate time to speak up and give out advice and second, there is also a time for keeping silent in order to gain a deeper understanding of the other person's world. While the majority of people don't struggle with holding back their opinion, listening to what someone else has to say can be far more challenging. If you have ever listened, to the extent that your entire being became utterly engrossed in the conversation, then you understand that this type of active listening requires intentionality and effort. It entails:

- Giving complete attention to the other person. The cell phone is turned off and schedule is cleared.
- Looking into the other person's eyes. The eyes have been described as the window to the soul. They provide a glimpse of what is going on in that person's inner world.
- Keeping an open, inviting posture with arms and legs uncrossed and your body turned toward theirs.

- Taking active involvement in the listening process by nodding in agreement and asking open-ended questions to draw out the other person.
- Keeping your feelings in alignment with the conversation. If a happy experience is being shared, you are smiling; if it's a sad experience, your eyes may begin to fill with tears.
- Being empathetic by trying to understand the other person's perspective and seeking to help them to feel heard and understood.

If you have ever been fortunate enough to have another person be with you in this manner, then you understand just how powerful it is. If you have ever been fully present with someone else, then you are well aware that this type of fervent listening requires a lot of energy, but it is also well worth the effort. Attentive listening is a way of giving others the gift of you, a gift of time, energy and undivided attention. It is one of the most valuable gifts that we can give. Client centered therapy demonstrates the power of being fully present with others and provides practical tools for putting this life-changing principle into action.

Person-Centered Therapy Basics

Person-centered therapy was founded by Carl Rogers, a man who understood the power of engaging in the moment. Person-centered therapy is unique in that it contains few therapeutic techniques and instead places the focus on becoming a healing presence. Roger's belief was that if the therapist demonstrated a specific set of qualities in his interactions with his clients, it would produce the necessary and sufficient conditions for growth to naturally occur. Rogers held this belief so intensely that he developed a unique, non-directive approach. Instead of providing solutions, Rogers would draw out his clients' ideas in a way that led them to generate their own answers to the problems that they faced. As clients continued to partner with the therapist in uncovering the solutions that were the best fit for them, they would come to see that they were fully capable of resolving their own troubles, which generated increased client confidence and independence.

These ideas were a revolutionary way of thinking in the field of psychology. Before Carl Rogers came along, the therapeutic process could be highly impersonal. The therapist's job was to remain a "blank slate" by injecting as little personality into the session as possible. Therapists were viewed as authority figures as opposed to partners in the process, and therapy placed higher value on the interventions used than on the relationship between the therapist and client. But this all changed with Carl Rogers, and as a result, Rogers came to be recognized as one of the top ten most eminent psychologists of the twentieth century and the second most influential clinician, exceeded only by Sigmund Freud himself.[2]

There is no doubt that Rogers made enormous contributions to the field of psychology as well as the world's understanding of relationships. According to Rogers there are only three things necessary for positive change to take place. These three key qualities are not therapeutic techniques, but ways of being that are openly lived out in the moment. These necessary and sufficient ingredients for change include empathy, congruence (or honest emotional expression) and unconditional positive regard. In addition to living out what he believed, Rogers also conducted extensive research, verifying his hypothesis. The research confirms that a strong bond between the therapist and client is a more reliable predictor of overall positive results than the specific techniques used during sessions.

Studies show that a positive client therapist relationship accounts for about 30 percent of therapeutic effectiveness, while technique accounts for only about 15 percent. Although both relationship and technique are important, when we are in a position where we must emphasize one, it's essential to remember "being" outshines "doing" every time, especially when it comes to empathy, congruence and unconditional positive regard.

But Roger's ideas are not only for therapists. They are vital skills for parents, pastors, teachers, mentors, friends, leaders and everyone longing to have a positive impact in the life of someone else. Let's take a closer look at how empathy, congruence and unconditional positive regard can help us be an influential, healing presence for others.

Increasing Empathy

Empathy is the capacity to view the world from someone else's perspective; it is "walking a mile in their shoes." The Apostle Paul writes about empathy in Romans 12:15 when he encourages believers to "Rejoice with those who rejoice, weep with those who weep." Empathy is essential when others are hurting because words hastily spoken compound the problem, but it's almost impossible to go wrong with empathy.

A Biblical Model of Empathy

A story of tremendous empathy is found in the book of Job. If you haven't come across it yet, the account is worth reading in its entirety, but the gist of the story goes like this: Job was an immensely wealthy man with a large family, a vast amount of property and plenty of livestock. Job honored God daily and was blessed by Him.

Then, one day Satan entered God's presence and accused Job of honoring Him only out of greed. Satan suggested that Job's motives were less than pure and nothing more than the natural result of the abundance God had given him. Satan proposed that Job's true colors would shine through if only he was allowed to put Job's faith to the test. God granted Satan's request and he immediately went to work. Through a series of sudden disasters, Job lost his children, his health and wealth, all in the same day.

When Job's three friends heard about the tragedy, they came to see him at once. Finding their friend lying in the dirt, covered with sores and in great anguish, they did something profoundly empathetic. According to the Bible, Job's friends "sat on the ground with him for seven days and seven nights. No one said a word to him, because they saw how great his suffering was."[2] Can you imagine what it would be like to sit with a friend for an entire week, mourning with him, yet never uttering a single word? Now that is empathy! Empathy can be provided in silence, through a soft look, tears and a gentle sigh. Empathy says, "I understand that you're hurting, and I hurt with you."

When demonstrating empathy, we may never fully understand the intricacies of what the other person is going through, and because of this, the words "I know how you feel," may not be appropriate. Nevertheless, each of us knows what it is like to be in pain and is able to empathize with the hurt the other person is experiencing. Another important point to remember is that empathy does not equal agreement. Sometimes people shy away from empathy, fearing that their compassion will be misinterpreted as a stamp of approval upon the other person's actions. But empathy does not equal approval. It is simply facing another person's pain with them.

In fact, as Job's story progresses, we find out that Job's friends don't see eye to eye with him at all, but are under the assumption that the calamity is his fault. After the seven days were up, these men spoke up, and as soon as they opened their mouths they got themselves into trouble. Job's friends accused him of secretly sinning against God, suggesting that hidden wrongdoings were the cause of this disaster. In spite of their initial astounding act of empathy, these so-called friends had the audacity to blame Job for bringing destruction upon himself.

As the story heads toward its conclusion, the three men are openly rebuked by God for the accusations they made. However, since the focus of this section is on empathy, I'll let you finish reading this narrative for yourself as we concentrate on what Job's friends did right. For seven days Job's friends held their tongues, empathizing with his sufferings, mourning his losses, and remaining present with him in the moment. Job's friends understood how to be with him in his pain and that is great empathy. This story also provides a sound warning for us when it comes to giving advice. Proverbs 10:19 says, "When words abound, transgression is inevitable." It's easy to get into trouble once we open our mouths, but almost impossible to go wrong with empathy.

Empathy Toward Ourselves

Just as it's important to show empathy toward others, it's equally as important to hold compassionate understanding toward ourselves. This involves accepting ourselves as we are, warts and all. While this may sound like an unusual concept, it's an important one. Some people are excellent at extending grace to others only to turn around and deal harshly with themselves. A lack of understanding of one's own humanness can lead to self-blaming and shaming, causing a person to become his or her own worst critic.

Therefore, it's vital that we extend to ourselves the same amount of compassionate understanding that we provide to others. The main thing to keep in mind is balance. At one extreme are those who extend too much grace to themselves and come to believe they are innocent of any wrongdoing. Of course, this is not good, and neither is the opposite extreme of becoming overly harsh with oneself. In a balanced approach, the motto becomes, "I'm not OK and you're not OK and that's OK." Imperfection in ourselves and others is expected and when we find ourselves guilty of wrongdoing, we acknowledge our mistakes, ask God for forgiveness, make amends whenever possible, and then move on. 2 Corinthians 3:18 says, "And we all... are being transformed into the same image from one degree of glory to another, which is from the Lord."

Transformation is an ongoing process in which we learn, and do the best we can with what we have as we move forward in our growth. Then, as we come to know better, we do better. Mistakes, errors in judgment and failing to get things right on the first try are all a natural part of this process. Just as it is important to empathize with others who are hurting, it is equally important to show compassionate understanding toward our own humanness by giving our selves permission to make mistakes.

Growing in Congruence

In high school geometry we learned that a congruent triangle is a shape in which all three sides match in length. Similarly, when we are congruent, what we feel on the inside matches with the emotions we are displaying on the outside. Someone who is congruent employs body language, facial expressions and a tone of voice that is consistent with their inner world. Simple examples of congruence include smiling when happy, tearing up when sad and letting out a sigh of exasperation. Some would refer to congruence as simply "being real." While congruence is a basic concept, it is not always easy to apply because being honest with others involves risk. Yet the risk is worth taking because congruence builds intimacy and trust.

James 1:8 speaks of a double-minded man who is unstable in all his ways. Incongruence is one sign of double-mindedness or mixed feelings about something. It is a warning light that signals that our words and emotions are not in agreement and is one indication that we may need to pause for a moment to better understand what is going on inside of us.

Congruence is vital in relationships because the majority of our communication takes place apart from the words that we speak. It's estimated that up to 90 percent of all the information we relay is nonverbal. One study concluded that 55 percent of meaning is drawn from body language, 38 percent from tone of voice, and only 7 percent from the actual words spoken. While exact percentages are still up for debate, there can be no doubt that our nonverbal communication is powerful.

A close friend of mine provided an excellent illustration of the power of congruence in relationships. This mom stands just over five feet tall and has two teenage sons who tower over her. Due to their size and athletic ability, these boys have the physical capacity to do anything they want at home, yet this particular mom has spent her entire life developing a close bond with her sons. These boys are securely attached to their mother, and mom is highly skilled in the area of non-verbal communication. Although this mother may no longer have the capacity to physically enforce the rules, she doesn't need to. She tells how, on multiple occasions, both of her boys have broken down in tears when she has given a look of disapproval. That is the power of congruent communication!

Contrast this with parents who have spent hours lecturing their children to no avail. Congruence magnifies the words we speak, making them much more meaningful than words alone. When words are not enough, congruence combined with a strong relationship is incredibly powerful.

Congruence is also consistent with a Biblical worldview. Jesus modeled congruent communication in his interaction with others. John 11:35, the shortest verse in the Bible, simply states that "Jesus wept." After hearing of the death of his dear friend Lazarus, Jesus sobbed deeply and those present responded by acknowledging Jesus' love for His friend. Words alone could never have relayed the intense compassion contained in those tears. Perhaps the reason the verse is so short is because so much meaning is compacted into that one small action.

Not only does congruence help us to better communicate, it also builds trust. In Matthew 21:28 Jesus told a story about two sons who were asked by their father to work in his vineyard. The first said, "I will not," but later changed his mind and went. The second answered, "I will, sir," but did not go. What's noteworthy about this parable is the eldest son's congruence. Initially deciding that he did not want to spend the day toiling in the sun, this young man provided an honest answer. Later, he changed his mind and did as his father asked. Now, contrast this with the second son, who said all of the right things but lacked the heart to follow through. How much better would it have been to say no when asked than to say yes and not show up?

At the conclusion of this story, the father knows that he can trust his older son to be honest with him. On the other hand, he also realizes that he needs to be wary when it comes to his younger son following through. In the end, the eldest son deserves double the credit: not only was he congruent, but he later re-evaluated his reply, changed his mind and did what his father asked. When we are honest in our relationships by communicating congruently, even when we know our genuine feelings are not what the other person would like to hear, it increases trust. As you can see from these examples, congruence is foundational to good communication.

Unconditional Positive Regard

The third concept emphasized by Carl Rogers is that of unconditional positive regard, or an authentic desire for the other person's best interest. This longing to see others succeed can be communicated through both verbal and non-verbal means. Unconditional positive regard was demonstrated by Jesus in Matthew 8:3 (NET), when He healed a man infected by leprosy. In Jesus' day, leprosy was an untreatable skin disease that would leave its victims scarred and disfigured before ending in death. The fear of contagion was so intense that those who contracted this disease were referred to as untouchables. The law commanded those with leprosy to warn approaching travelers by yelling the phrase "unclean, unclean" as a way of cautioning them to keep their distance.

One day, while Jesus and his disciples were traveling, a man blemished and gnarled by this life-threatening illness called out, asking to be healed. While Jesus could have stayed far away and cured this man with a spoken word, a common way that he'd healed others in the past, instead Jesus "reached out his hand and touched the man. 'I am willing,' he said. 'Be clean!' Immediately he was cleansed of his leprosy."[5] Jesus demonstrated unconditional positive regard by providing a tender touch that communicated loud and clear, "Though others may see you as untouchable, I do not!"

Jesus then went on to express the ultimate act of unconditional positive regard by laying down His life on the cross. Romans 5:8 (Net) says, "But God demonstrates his own love for us in this: While we were still sinners, Christ died for us." Notice that God didn't wait for you and me to clean up our act before displaying His love, and there is not even a requirement to meet Him halfway. God's love for you and I comes with no strings attached.

Unconditional positive regard unceasingly desires the best for others. It remains hopeful, always believing that change is possible. For Christ followers this should be easy because every person we come in contact with holds great worth. A $100 bill provides a tremendous illustration of the value of those around us. If I were to take a new, crisp $100 bill out of my wallet, that bill would be worth exactly $100, the value assigned to it by the National Treasury. If I were to take that same $100 bill, crumple it up, throw it on the ground and stomp on it, though tattered, that bill would still be worth exactly $100. The fact that the bill is untidy and muddled does nothing to change its worth.

Similarly, everyone you and I come in contact with has incredible significance assigned to them by God. This value is the price paid by Jesus Christ on that cross. John 3:16 (NET) says, "For this is the way God loved the world: He gave his one and only Son, so that everyone who believes in him will not perish but have eternal life." Like a $100 bill, everyone we come in contact with has an assigned worth that cannot be changed. When we provide unconditional positive regard to others, we are treating them as the valuable person they truly are.

Connections That Lead to Change

Empathy, congruence and unconditional positive regard are powerful tools that serve as a catalyst for positive change. These three qualities allow us to connect to others and create a healing environment where growth occurs naturally. All of us have people we would like to influence. In order to do this in a way that doesn't raise resentment it's always best to start with these three ingredients. The value of using relationships to promote positive changes in others has been proclaimed in a variety of different ways. Here are three of my favorites:

> *"Nobody cares how much you know, until they know how much you care."*

This quote has been attributed to a number of different sources including leadership expert John Maxwell and President Theodore Roosevelt. In order to lead and influence others well, we must first demonstrate that we care. When I began my journey of going back to school, the first class I took was taught by our seminary dean. This was the same dean who put his schedule on hold to help me get started in my new career. Knowing that he cared about me made an enormous impact in the way that I approached the courses I took. I was motivated to do my best and willing to move outside of my comfort zone because I truly believed that the dean, and the seminary in general, had my best interest at heart. A year after graduating, when I was asked to return as an adjunct professor, I jumped at the opportunity. I was thrilled to be a part of an institution that cared so much about me when I was a student and am honored to be able to pass on this legacy of genuine compassion to new students entering the program.

> *"Rules without relationship lead to rebellion."*

I first heard these words spoken by Christian author and apologist Josh McDowell and have seen this statement ring true time and time again in my work with families. The teen years can be especially difficult, and quite often the difference between teenagers who thrive at home and those who spend the majority of this time in and out of juvenile hall is the relationship between these teens and other significant adults in their lives. Parents, teachers, coaches, youth pastors and mentors all have the ability to build positive relationships that add credibility to the structure society has put in place.

For example, a teenage boy may care little about getting arrested and might even view this as a way of gaining status among his peers. However, many teens would cringe at the thought of seeing their mother cry, and hearing their father speak the words, "I'm really disappointed right now," as well as shudder at the thought of letting down the entire football team due to misbehavior that prevented them from playing in the big game.

Ephesians 6:4 says, "Fathers, do not provoke your children to anger, but raise them up in the discipline and instruction of the Lord." For parents, empathy, congruence and unconditional positive regard are valuable because they create a bond that guides children toward making wise decisions. Strong relationships are the key to effective discipline, while rules without a relationship only add to the problem.

*"Children may forget what you say to them,
but they will never forget how you make them
feel."*

While I was serving as an intern at a local church, these words were posted on the door of our children's ministry department. Although this quote speaks specifically of children, it's applicable to everyone. Long after teachings, lectures, scolding and instructions are forgotten, others will remember how they felt while they were in our presence. This principle is particularly useful for those who are married. Husbands and wives know the words "I love you," alone are not sufficient and must be backed up with actions.

Studies place a three-to-one ratio for positive versus negative interactions in relationships, showing that it takes approximately three positive exchanges to make up for one negative one. When our significant others feel good about themselves when they are around us approximately 75 percent of the time, the foundation is laid for a healthy, lasting relationship. Using this three-to-one formula, relationship expert John Gottman has been able to predict with over 90 percent accuracy which relationships will last and which will fail after observing couples for as little as five minutes. It's not so much the words that we speak, but more importantly, how we make the other person feel when they are in our presence that causes our relationships to last.

As you can see, who we are really is more important than the tasks we accomplish. Person- centered therapy teaches us that character and love for others will be remembered long after our words are forgotten. Right now is a great time to begin laying the foundation for close, lasting relationships through empathy, congruence and unconditional positive regard.

Life Lessons from Person-centered Therapy

Close, lasting relationships are fostered through empathy, congruence, and unconditional positive regard.

Questions for Additional Reflection and Discussion

1. Think of a time when someone gave you their full and undivided attention while listening to you in an empathetic and caring manner. What was it like for you to have someone listen to you like this?

2. Is it hard for you to show empathy toward people who are hurting but also taking actions to cause their own painful situation? Why or why not?

3. Are you empathetic toward your own situations or do you tend to be more judgmental and harsh with yourself than with others? If so, how will you begin fostering empathy toward yourself this week?

4. Do you find it easy to be congruent and say what you mean or is this something that is more difficult for you? Why do you think this comes easily/is more challenging for you?

5. Do you find it easy or difficult to show unconditional positive regard toward people who seemingly don't deserve it? How does understanding Christ's love for us make showing unconditional positive regard for others easier?

6. Who do you know who needs extra grace extended to them? How can you reach out to them with empathy congruence and unconditional positive regard this week? Give a specific example of what doing this would look like.

Seven

Letting Down Our Defenses:

Life Lessons from Psychoanalysis

Men are more moral than they think and far
more immoral than they can imagine.

~ *Sigmund Freud*

And it's clear enough, isn't it, that we're sinners,
every one of us, in the same sinking boat with
everybody else?

~ Romans 6:19, *The Message*

Freud concluded that mankind tends to
self-sabotage—a belief very much in
alignment with Scripture—and he came
to this belief through the use of science
and observation alone.

A n examination of life's greatest lessons from psychology and Scripture wouldn't be complete without diving into the works of Sigmund Freud, the father of modern psychology, and his contribution of classic psychoanalysis. When it comes to biblical integration, psychoanalysis presents a number of strengths, in addition to some unique challenges. In the courses I teach at the seminary, I always begin by asking students, "What questions do you have about psychology?" I've received many answers over the years, but the one response that consistently arises is, "I want to know how and if the Bible and psychology are compatible with one another." While the exact phrasing varies, the inquiry itself is always the same.

What I have found is that, quite often, Christ followers have nagging doubts about the appropriateness of applying tools from psychology to their daily lives. Hopefully by now you have seen for yourself how psychology and the Bible work together, hand in hand, in many areas. Yet, for others, persistent doubts remain — doubts that can often be traced back to Sigmund Freud and classic psychoanalysis.

These conflicts have led some to quickly glance over Freud's works and others to discard them completely. However, I would suggest a more productive approach. Studying Freud is much like studying the biblical Old Testament. While the Old Testament is filled with immense wisdom, it also contains traditions, laws, regulations and stories that do not accurately reflect how Christianity is currently lived out. Today, Christ followers are not under the Mosaic Law, but under grace. The Old Testament law was a better structure than everything that preceded it, but pales in comparison to the grace and freedom we currently have in Jesus Christ. Although the law was good, it was only the beginning of a much grander plan.

In a similar manner, Freud's work is the start of something much larger. Classic psychoanalysis served as a catalyst that brought much needed attention to the value of relationships and the importance of attending to mental health needs. This process that began with Freud continued to develop over time, leading to increased compassion for those who suffer and creating vast improvements in the mental health care system. As we will see, at times, the journey from where psychology was to where it is today has been messy, but the progress has been well worth the effort.

It's important to understand that Freud was a pioneer in his field who, like many pioneers, got just about as many things wrong as he did right. Because of this, Freud's works are best approached by using a biblical filter that allows us to hold on to the valuable pieces of his work while sifting out the parts that are less relevant, and we will practice doing this throughout the chapter.

The Birth of Modern Psychology

Freud was born on May 6, 1856 in *Freiberg in Mähren,* a small town in the Czech Republic. He was the eldest of eight children and an excellent student who graduated from high school with honors. Because Freud was such an avid reader of Shakespeare, some have theorized that his interest in human relationships was inspired by these works. In 1881 Freud began his career as medical doctor at the University of Vienna. Later, he would return to his alma matter to serve as a university lecturer and professor.

In October 1885, the course of Freud's life drastically changed when he began studying under a renowned neurologist conducting research in hypnosis. Freud's friend and mentor in hypnosis, Josef Breuer, had a client by the name of Anna O, who was invited to talk about her symptoms while under this relaxed state. During these sessions, Anna would mutter words and phrases about whatever thoughts came into her mind. Anna referred to this process of freely speaking her mind as "chimney sweeping," and attributed this "talking cure" to the lessening of her symptoms.

Freud observed all of this, and after a time of integrating hypnosis into his own practice, theorized that a consistent course of treatment could be provided without its use. Freud built on the idea of "chimney sweeping" and used key components as the framework for free association. By 1896, Freud was implementing the foundational ideas of psychoanalysis, including the connection between unconscious, repressed desires and the symptoms his patients experienced. In order to help his patients access their unconscious, Freud delved deeper into dream exploration, (which he called "the royal road to the unconscious"), free association, and the exploration of sexual drives and desires.

From Freud's story, there are two things that stand out. First, we see that psychoanalysis developed out of a need. Freud observed people in mental anguish who had no clear path to healing. He sought to meet this need by providing a dependable approach to treatment. Second, it's important to note that the methods of treatment that were available at the time were broad, ranging from hypnosis to mental institutions, so in forging a new path Freud had to rely heavily on a process of trial and error.

But forging new ground had a cost—it created significant controversy. As we examine Freud's life, there are flashes of pure genius, as well as moments that cause us to groan because, in his eagerness to help, some huge mistakes were made along the way. While some of these errors were immediately identified, others were filtered out gradually in the decades that followed. In the end, Freud's work is a conglomeration of the good, the bad and the downright weird, but it's encouraging to know that valuable lessons can be gleaned from all of it.

The Good, the Bad and the Weird

Psychology teaches us that when something strange is going on, it is best to acknowledge its presence. When it comes to Freud, there are some character issues and theological discrepancies that are beyond repair. In this book, we will manage these inconsistencies by acknowledging they exist, choosing to view them as an important part of the development of modern-day psychology and moving on.

One obvious example of the strange in Freud's work is his stance on cocaine use, which included his personal use of the drug. In 1884, Freud wrote a paper entitled "On Coca," where he extolled the virtues of this narcotic. During the next four years Freud built upon his hypothesis with a number of articles talking about cocaine's benefits as an antidepressant, and even went so far as to recommend its use as a cure for morphine addiction. These endorsements led to a tarnished medical reputation from which Freud never fully recovered. Although he eventually stopped recommending the drug, Freud continued occasional use himself.

While this is most certainly an example of poor decision-making on Freud's part, before becoming overly critical, there are some additional factors to keep in mind. First, Freud grew up in an era where a multitude of new discoveries were being made, and interestingly enough, Freud was not the only one to show poor judgment in the area of cocaine use. Coca-Cola's original formula included extracts from the coca leaf, causing this product to, at one time, contain an estimated nine milligrams of cocaine in every glass. Of course, this has long since been removed from the modern-day formula, but this didn't happen until 1901, after Coca-Cola had been on the market for a number of years. Our society has certainly come a long way in the last century!

Although Freud is guilty of errors in judgment, these faults by no means define his work. Other aspects are pure genius. When it comes to Freud's identification of defense mechanisms and the power of the unconscious, psychoanalysis has much to offer, and we will examine both of these areas later on in this chapter.

The first leadership lesson that we learn from Freud comes from Freud's life itself. Good leaders are quick to test everything as opposed to rushing in and believing what they hear. Wise Christ followers put 1

Thessalonians 5:21-22 into practice. This Scripture exhorts believers to "examine all things; hold fast to what is good. Stay away from every form of evil." This sound advice has applications for every aspect of life because rarely do events present themselves in black-and-white ways. If they did, discernment would be easy. Christ followers would have no problems in labeling things as "good" and "bad," then moving on. But we live in a world where black and white are intermingled with shades of grey and God has left us with the responsibility of using the sound minds He has given us to separate the helpful from unhelpful.

Thriving in the Grey Zone

Life in the grey-zone is all about learning to thrive in a world where good and evil are intermingled and difficult to distinguish. Jesus told a parable about this in Matthew 13:24-30. In this parable, a farmer planted his field with wheat. Then, at night, an enemy, quite possibly a neighboring farmer with a competing wheat field, snuck in and scattered weeds among the crops. By the time the servants realized what had happened, it was too late. The weeds had sprouted and the damage was done.

In a state of panic, the servants informed the farmer of the events that transpired and requested to begin pulling out the weeds immediately. But the wise farmer slowed the servants down by declining their suggestion for immediate intervention. The farmer knew that these particular weeds, called tares, looked very much like wheat until fully grown. If the servants rushed to pull them up, they would end up unintentionally uprooting the good crop in the process. Instead, the farmer instructed his servants to allow both the wheat and the weeds to grow together until the harvest. At this time, distinguishing between the two would be easy, but until then, the wheat and tares would be allowed to grow side by side.

This parable is packed with meaning for us today. On that glorious day when Christ returns, good and evil will once and for all be separated but until then, we live in a world where both are present and not always easily distinguishable. Because of this, sound judgment is necessary in all aspects of life. The good, bad and strange of life are everywhere; not even Christian culture has escaped its grasp. There is no shortage of Bible teachers who are swift to take the word of God out of context, from late-night television preachers who promise miracles for a small fee, to passionate leaders who are very sincere in their theology but, nevertheless, sincerely wrong.

Two unfortunate extremes can result from living in a world where the wheat and weeds are so closely intermingled. One error is to disregard the good because of the bad. This is what would have happened if the farmer allowed his servants to immediately pluck out the weeds. On one hand, the weeds would have been eliminated, but on the other hand, much of this farmer's good crop would have been damaged in the process.

One example of rushing in to pull out the weeds happens when Christ followers disregard psychology entirely. It's true that those who do this protect themselves from some of the errors it contains, but the downside is that they also miss out on the many benefits psychology has to offer. As someone raised in a homeschooling environment during the last two-and-a-half years of high school, I witnessed many families over-shelter their children from worldly evils, only to have their good intentions backfire later on. Friends I grew up with who were sheltered from the "weeds of life" during their teen years found themselves ill-equipped to function in the world of reality as an adult. This is another example of rushing in to pull the "weeds" to the detriment of the overall "crop." While these families succeeded in protecting their children from worldly vices, in the process, many teachable moments were missed and sound judgment was not passed on, resulting in problems that surfaced in adulthood.

The second extreme involves unpretentiously following a teaching or teacher without question. All too often, people latch on to leaders or belief systems and naively follow them to their own detriment. From a biblical perspective, nothing should be beyond inquiry. The Bible calls believers to an intelligent faith. The Apostle Paul praised a group of people from the city of Berea because, when he preached in this city, the residents did not take Paul at his word, but instead searched the Scriptures daily to confirm that what he taught was true.[1]

We live in an era where there is more access to information than ever before. Like the Bereans, we must learn to come to the Scriptures on a continual basis in order to sift out the wheat from the weeds. From Freud we are reminded of the values of testing everything, applying to our lives that which is good and getting rid of the junk. In examining psychoanalysis, we want to be sure neither to place Freud on a pedestal nor to view him as a villain. Instead, it's helpful to picture Freud as a pioneer who was at times misguided, while at others a prodigy in his field. Now that we have examined the important leadership and relational lessons that can be gleaned from the mistakes made, let's move on to the areas in which Freud excelled.

The Visible and Invisible Worlds Around Us

Freud was a determinist. This means that he viewed humanity as possessing limited freedom. Freud believed that the decisions we make are heavily influenced by unconscious motivations and biological drives. Perhaps you have seen Freud's "iceberg" model where the tip of the iceberg peeks above the water's surface while the majority of the icy mass is submerged out of sight. A lack of awareness of the accumulation below the surface is what sunk the Titanic, and according to psychoanalysis, it is a similar lack of awareness that sinks us. In Freud's model, the tip of the iceberg represents the conscious mind, or that part of our inner drive that we are aware of. The much larger, submerged part represents the unconscious, or the parts of us that heavily influence our actions yet remain hidden. This unconscious part of our mind leaks out in dreams, manifests in unintended marks of the pen and reveals itself through slips of the tongue — also known as the Freudian slip.

The idea that there is much more happening in our world than we are aware of is consistent with a biblical worldview. In the previous chapter, we got a glimpse of these unseen forces at work though the life of Job. Job's troubles came as a result of an invisible conflict in the heavens. Like Job, you and I dwell in the midst of a heavenly battle. The Bible describes Satan as real, active and stalking his prey like a roaring lion. Like Job, you and I are impacted by events outside of our understanding.

The idea of determinism is also found in the Bible. It is written about by the Apostle Paul who acknowledged these unseen influences impacting his life when he wrote, "For I don't understand what I am doing. For I do not do what I want - instead, I do what I hate.[2]" Most of us can relate to this all too well. Perhaps there is a goal we are striving to accomplish or a habit we want to break. Intellectually we know the steps that need to be taken, yet in spite of having the necessary understanding and the desire to change, we continue to find ourselves taking contradictory actions. Anyone who has ever broken a New Year's resolution, strayed from their diet for a guilty, fast-food pleasure, replaced studying for an exam with a late night out with friends, or neglected prayer, Bible study and connecting with God due to getting caught up in the hustle and bustle of life knows what this is like. Like the Apostle Paul, we know the good that we ought to do, and long to do it, but somehow find ourselves engaged in just the opposite. Determinism suggests that we do not have as much control over our life as we would like to think.

Moving Past Our Defenses

Freud understood the depravity of the human condition and described it well. Not only do we become experts at averting good, we also play all sorts of games to hide from pain and responsibilities. The tools and techniques we use to deceive ourselves are creative and abundant. While obstacles are a normal part of life, no one hinders our progress more than the person gazing back at us on the other side of the mirror. Freud described this tendency to self-sabotage in terms of defense mechanisms. Each defense mechanism has the benefit of helping us to avoid some pain, but this comes at the high price of distorting reality. Although viewing the world through the lens of defense mechanisms is an easier pill to swallow, this false reality thwarts us from getting to the root of our problems. In the end, defense mechanisms over-promise, under-deliver, and prevent lasting healing from taking place.

Defense mechanisms can best be described as maladaptive tools used outside of one's awareness. Freud placed a high priority on making the unconscious conscious because he understood that positive changes occur as awareness increases. 1 Peter 2:9 states that God calls believers "out of darkness and into His marvelous light." Shining a light on the defense mechanisms by increasing our awareness of these harmful behavior patterns is the first step toward letting our defenses down. As we examine the following defense mechanisms, see if you can identify times where these patterns may have been present in your life.

Repression

In repression, a person disguises threatening impulses, thoughts and desires by pushing them out of conscious awareness. Repression is at the root of all of the defense mechanisms, and according to Freud, the ability to repress is always incomplete.

When I was a child, during the beginning of each summer, my dad would spend hours setting up a temporary swimming pool in our back yard. This pool was about four feet deep, and although it was nothing fancy, it was the perfect way to keep cool during the hot

California summer, as well as a popular attraction for the neighborhood kids. One game we played involved attempting to submerge an inflated beach ball. The goal was to see if we could push the ball all the way to the bottom of the pool. If you've ever tried this, then you know it's not an easy task. The beach ball is always trying to resurface and the further underwater the ball is pushed, the heavier it feels.

However, with a little practice, my friends and I became quite good at working as a team to push our fully inflated beach ball to the bottom, where we would hold it firmly pressed to the floor. Then the real fun began. Someone would begin the countdown, "Three... two... one!" The submerged ball would be released, quickly forcing its way to the surface where it would shoot out of the water, much to our delight. The thing about a submerged beach ball is that it can't stay underwater forever. Like a child attempting to push down a beach ball in a swimming pool, our repressed desires eventually force their way up. This can occur through dreams, slips of the tongue and negative patterns of behavior.

One of my college professors used to say, "That which we suppress, we magnify,[3]" meaning, the deeper we push down feelings of anger, frustration and sorrow, the more intensely these feelings will rocket to the surface. As someone who has spent time working with children with extensive trauma histories I can attest to this. I've witnessed temper tantrums occur over seemingly insignificant events. For example, a two- or three-minute time-out might trigger an hour of flailing and crying. Parents have shared how what was thought was a minor disappointment resulted in their teenage son or daughter bursting into tears and running away from home. In instances like these, when the reaction is far above what would be considered age-appropriate and normal for the situation, the response is not really about the event at all. Instead, the event is a trigger that brought to the surface all of the repressed feelings submerged inside.

Adults do this too. It's likely that at some point you will come in contact with a person who displays emotions that are far more intense than the situation calls for. When this happens, it's easy to take that person's reaction personally and wonder, "What did I do to upset him or her so much?" But these emotions are not really about you. Whenever a person's emotions are grossly exaggerated, it says more about what is going on inside of that person than it does about you.

In fact, intense feelings are a lot like gunpowder. Stuff enough gunpowder into a barrel and the tiniest spark will result in a massive explosion. In a similar manner, when feelings are repressed, they get packed tightly inside of a person over time. Eventually the tiniest spark unleashes an enormous emotional eruption. Now contrast this with the emotionally healthy individual who, instead of repressing his feelings, releases them in small doses through the day. Therapists refer to these acts of release as coping skills.

Coping skills are best described as any healthy means of reducing stress. They include activities such as working out, talking to close friends, prayer, meditation, enjoyable hobbies and confronting problems directly as they arise. The person who practices positive coping skills on a regular basis is taking their "gunpowder" and safely dispersing it over time. Let's go back to the previous illustration, and this time take that exact same barrel of gunpowder and picture it spread out evenly over a vast, empty parking-lot (warning... don't actually try this at home!!!). A triggering event happens, igniting the powder and this time there is a.... "poof" and that's it. The powder fizzles, releasing a puff of smoke, but no bang, no explosion, no trauma and drama, and most importantly, no damage done to the relationship.[4] As you can see, repression is dangerous because it leads to explosions. What we stuff deep inside continues to impact us, and one day, it will bubble to the surface.

A second danger of repression is that it is deceptive. Jesus referred to the religious leaders of his day as "whitewashed tombs.[5]" On the outside the Pharisees appeared good, clean and spiritual. They would bind scriptures to various parts of their body in leather pouches called phylacteries and exceeded the expectations of the Mosaic Law by tithing from their herbs and spices. But while the Pharisees possessed a religious poise, they lacked true spirituality. According to Jesus, these men were dead on the inside and this deadness leaked out in their interactions with others.

Although they put on a good show, the Pharisees were well known for their harsh judgments. They had no mercy for those who did not appear as outwardly spiritual as themselves. The inward deadness of the Pharisees showed in their hypocrisy. They were not flawless, only experts at disguising their faults. They became so good at this that they managed to suppress their wrongdoings out of their own awareness as well. This is precisely what repression does: it hinders us from recognizing and dealing with our own "stuff," causing us to remain ignorant and stagnant. The Pharisees' actions serve as a warning for us because, if we are not cautious, we can just as easily fall into a similar pattern. But repression is just the beginning. There are many other creative ways that you and I keep the illusion going by hiding our faults from ourselves.

Rationalization

Rationalization is another tool of self-deception. It's what Adam and Eve did in the Garden of Eden when they saw that the fruit was "good for food, pleasing to the eye, and desirable for gaining wisdom.[6]" Instead of trusting God, Adam and Eve invented reasons to do things their own way. Rationalization says, "God must be wrong, something that looks so good can't be bad." It's the same type of logic used by young children who gorge themselves on candy only to feel sick a short time later.

Rationalization can be powerful. My most vivid memory of the firm grasp rationalization can have on a person occurred in an addiction recovery group I led during my counseling internship. One particular man in the group had been court-ordered to participate in the program due to an ongoing drinking problem. In spite of a number of DUIs resulting in his arrest, the loss of his career and broken trust with his family, this man continued to insist that alcoholism was not an issue. Instead, he bemoaned having to go through the recovery process to please the courts. He could not grasp what other men in the group saw clearly and when confronted always found a way to rationalize and dismiss what was being said. "But that was only a one-time event," he would say, or "Yes, my drinking got me in trouble then too, but I can still quit whenever I want." No amount of logic would cause this man to change his mind — rationalization had him in its rock-solid grasp. My hope was that through time, and the power of the group process, this barrier would eventually be broken down.

Like Adam and Eve, this man saw the "forbidden fruit," rationalized and partook. This story of Adam and Eve would be much more pleasant if it were only about Adam and Eve. If we are honest with ourselves, avoiding rationalization, we too will have to admit guilt in one area or another. 1 John 1:8 says that if a person says they have no sin, they are only deceiving themselves. Like Adam and Eve, all of us have strayed from God's perfect plan. Letting go of rationalization necessitates admitting and taking responsibility for our faults. Like a surgery that begins in pain and ends in healing, gaining awareness of our own shortcomings hurts, but leads to restoration.

Displacement

Displacement is a defense mechanism where a person diverts intense feelings away from one source to a more acceptable scapegoat. For example, a man upset at his boss due to being overlooked for a promotion might take out his frustration on his family because home seems like a safer venue in which to vent. At work, disciplinary actions and a human resource department are in place to manage inappropriate outbursts, whereas this man may believe his family will be more likely to overlook his anger.

We also find displacement in Eden. When God questions Adam about eating the forbidden fruit, instead of accepting responsibility for his actions, he points the finger, stating, "The woman you put here with me — she gave me some fruit from the tree, and I ate it.⁷" In a single breath, Adam displaces his guilt by pointing the finger at Eve and God. Although it's easy to criticize Adam, is there anyone who hasn't moved their feelings of anger, blame and guilt to a more acceptable source? Displacement happens when we have a bad day and then turn around and snap at our children. It occurs when we get angry at a teacher for a failing grade instead of owning the responsibility ourselves, and when we blame conflict in marriage on our spouse being unreasonable while overlooking our own contributions. In displacement, attention is diverted off of ourselves and onto a more acceptable culprit.

Reaction Formation

Reaction formation occurs when someone tries to make reality appear the opposite of what it really is. For example, a person feeling timid inside might attempt to compensate by wearing a rough outer exterior, as is often the case with the school bully. While bullies are quick to pick on others, they are often deeply wounded themselves. As the old saying goes, "Hurt people, hurt people," and sometimes those with hurting hearts put on the toughest exteriors.

Reaction formation is what causes a drug user to put a MADD (Mothers against Drunk Driving) sticker on the back of her car and a pastor with a pornography addiction to passionately preach against its vices during the Sunday morning sermon. Reaction formation is hypocritical, a showy way of pretending to be something that we are not.

Scriptural support for this defense mechanism takes us out of the Genesis story and all the way to the other end of the Bible. In Revelations 3:17, the Apostle Paul writes to the church at Laodicea, stating, "You say, 'I am rich; I have acquired wealth and do not need a thing.' But you do not realize that you are wretched, pitiful, poor, blind and naked." In reaction formation, a person who is broke spends like they are rich and a church that is morally bankrupt will proclaim themselves a saint. A person who acts as if they are in a right standing with God because their good deeds outweigh their bad is also demonstrating characteristics of reaction formation. Those who believe this have adopted a form of spiritual tunnel vision by honing in on their positive aspects while ignoring the negative. A sign of health is the ability to acknowledge both our desirable and undesirable parts. But this can be difficult to do when the defense mechanism of denial is so much more comfortable.

Denial

Out of all of the defense mechanisms, denial may be the most damaging. Denial refuses to acknowledge that any problem exists. This can be seen in the woman in a physically abusive relationship who insists that everything is just fine. Black eyes and broken bones are explained away through stories that don't make logical sense. In spite of the glaring physical evidence, the victim adamantly maintains that no real problem is present. But these stories are more for the victim's benefit than for anyone else. In denial, the words, "He hit me" are too difficult to say. To admit this would mean acknowledging the current way of doing things is not working, confronting the problem head-on, and moving toward change. Change can be scary, and for some people, refusing to acknowledge the reality of the problem is far more comfortable.

Denial was used by the Pharisees in the New Testament when they refused to recognize their own sinfulness. Their denial ran so deep that it was less painful for them to crucify Jesus than to listen to Him proclaim the world's need for a savior. If you and I claim that we are good and without the need of a savior, then we too are guilty of denial. Denial is an ongoing way people deceive themselves and what makes denial so dangerous is that those in a state of true denial are not fully aware of what they are doing.

Our Psychological Family

The defense mechanisms paint a bleak picture of the human condition. Fortunately Freud didn't end his work with their discovery. His answer to the problem of defense mechanisms is twofold. First, he sought to make the unconscious conscious. Becoming aware of our defenses is the first step in moving past them. His second goal was to strengthen the ego. Freud divided the personality into three parts consisting of the id, the ego and the superego. The id operates on the pleasure principle. It's the part of us that wants what it wants, when it wants it. If the id were a family member, it would best be described as the baby of the family. The id says, "If it feels good, do it," and urges us to find pleasure in the here and now regardless of future consequences. The id aches for immediate gratification.

On the other end of the spectrum is the superego, which focuses on morals and internalized ideals. It is sometimes referred to as the conscience and it keeps us informed of how things should be. If the superego were a family member, it would be the pastor of the family. The positive of the superego is that it is an altruistic part of us that leads us toward acting compassionately. The down side is that, when unchecked, the superego becomes reckless and judgmental. Those with an overactive superego can become so concerned with the ideal picture of how things should be that they don't plan for the future, such as the case of someone donating to a meaningful cause only to find that they have nothing to live on themselves. The other problem with an overactive superego is that it can be judgmental, condemning those with different belief systems and those who do not share similar passion for a cause. Although the superego has many benefits, like the ego, it can also wreak havoc if left unbridled.

Finally, there is the ego, the professor of the family. The ego focuses on the reality principle and mediates between the desires of the id and superego. The ego is logical and seeks out truth. A strong ego will prevent the id from gorging itself in acts of immediate gratification while still allowing a person to enjoy pleasure. It is the ego that reminds us eating one piece of candy is fine but eating ten pieces will make us feel sick. The ego also brings balance to the superego. During times when we are tempted to judge others too harshly, the ego brings to our attention that we too are human and have failed in the past. The ego allows us to disagree with others without becoming overtly harsh and condemning. It's interesting that, although a staunch atheist, Freud came to the conclusion that humanity has a tendency to self-sabotage — a belief very much in alignment with a biblical world view — and he came to this discovery through the use of observation and scientific research alone.

Seeking Truth

Freud was an avid seeker of truth who desired to help people see the world as it really is. As Freud grew older, his harsh judgment of faith began to soften. Freud passed away on September 23, 1939 at the age of 83. My theory, and yes, this is only a theory, is that the more Freud sought out truth, the more he was pointed in the direction of Christ. I can't help but wonder if Freud had lived another hundred years, whether his love of truth would have led him to the one who said, "I am the way, the truth and the life.[8]"

In examining Freud's work, it appears that, at times, he was close to this. He certainly had the first part of the gospel message down. Romans 3:23 says, "For all have sinned and fall short of the glory of God." The defense mechanisms demonstrate mankind's exceptional creativity in keeping one's sinfulness out of conscious awareness. While the id and superego provide examples of mankind's depravity as evidenced through his tendency to fall into excessive indulgence and self-righteous judging, the ego reveals the value of truth, another key biblical concept. In John 8:32, Jesus said, "You will know the truth, and the truth will set you free." To follow Christ is to be a seeker of truth. Jesus calls His followers to step out of darkness and into the light by letting down their defenses, acknowledging past failures, and dealing with them directly through His work on the cross.

The foundational message of the Bible is summed up in 1 Corinthians 15:3-4 where Paul writes, "For I passed on to you as of first importance what I also received–that Christ died for our sins according to the scriptures, and that he was buried, and that he was raised on the third day according to the scriptures." The message of the Bible is simple: we've all done wrong things that separate us from God. God doesn't want this separation so He sent His son, Jesus, to pay the penalty of our sins and take the punishment for our wrongdoings in our place. Following Christ involves putting our faith in the work on the cross as payment for our wrongdoings, as opposed to trusting any actions on our part.

If you have chosen to trust Jesus as your connection point to God, you are a follower of Christ. After dying, Jesus rose from the dead three days later, showing the world that He is Lord over life, death and everything else. One day Christ will return and make everything wrong with the world right. Until then, He calls us to be ongoing seekers of truth and living examples of His grace, love and mercy. Embracing Christ is the ultimate form of strengthening the ego. In classic psychoanalysis, we learn to recognize our weakness and manage them rationally by stepping out of unawareness as we firmly grasp the light of truth.

Life Lessons from Psychoanalysis

We can be good at deceiving ourselves. Life is better when we let down our defenses, seek truth, and come to the one who is "the way, the truth and the life."

Questions for Additional Reflection and Discussion

1. Many people have some knowledge of Freud and his works. Which parts of his theories bother you and which ones get you excited?

2. Have you seen the defense mechanisms lived out in the lives of others and what result did utilizing the defense mechanisms have?

3. Which defense mechanisms do you find yourself using most often? Why do you think you use this one, what purpose does it serve?

4. What do you think of the idea of coming to Christ as a way of dealing with a person's sinful condition?

5. Have you made the decision to put your faith in Christ for forgiveness? Why or why not?

Eight

Discovering Meaning:

Life Lessons from Existential Theory

Ever more people today have the means to live,
but no meaning to live for.

~ Viktor Frankl

A painful past doesn't necessitate a tainted future. Through God's grace and persistent determination, negative circumstances can become a catalyst for dynamic growth

Friedrich Nietzsche, a well-known German philosopher and poet declared, "He who has a *why* to live can bear with most any *how*." This was a favorite saying of existential therapist Viktor Frankl, a man who discovered his *why* and as a result, was able to move forward and thrive after having survived some of the most excruciating circumstances. Viktor was born on March 25, 1905, in Vienna, Austria where he was the second of three children. His parents were poor civil servants, and during the First World War, when Viktor was only nine years old, he and his family experienced bitter depravation. Basic necessities were so scarce that Viktor and his siblings would travel to neighboring farmhouses to beg for food. Yet, in spite of his meager beginnings, Viktor took an active role in forging his own path. He displayed an interest in psychology from an early age and attended lectures on applied psychology while still in high school.

After graduating, Viktor continued his education at the University of Vienna where he specialized in neurology and psychiatry before going on to serve as the director of the neurological department at Rothschild Hospital. Things were looking up until suddenly, on September 25, 1942, when Viktor was only two years into his directorship and thirty-seven years old, everything changed. It was an era of extreme racial prejudice and due to his Jewish heritage, Viktor, along with his wife, parents, and siblings, were deported to a Nazi ghetto. Life in the ghetto was harsh, and the standard of living steadily declined in the years that followed.

Viktor, however, continued to put his clinical expertise to good use. Although he was initially assigned a job as a general medical practitioner, after demonstrating his skills in mental health, he was transferred to a psychiatric care unit where he organized therapeutic groups that supported newcomers in adjusting to the overwhelming shock of ghetto life. Viktor played a key role in forming suicide watch groups and designed a series of lectures to assist the community in remaining mentally sound amid the ongoing uncertainty.

Then, on October 19, 1944, things again took a turn for the worst. Viktor was deported to Auschwitz, a Nazi concentration camp known for its harsh conditions and extreme brutality. Shortly after arriving, Viktor and the other detainees experienced a new level of degradation as they were stripped of their personal belongings, including watches, wedding bands, and all but a single layer of clothing. Their heads were shaved and numbers were tattooed on their bodies. Amongst the guards, Viktor was no longer referred to by his name, but was known as number 119,104 and regarded as less than human. He was assigned to a manual labor unit laying tracks for the railroad, his meals consisted of a meager serving of bread and watered-down soup, and brutal beatings by the guards became a daily norm. Over the next eighteen months, Viktor was shuffled from one overcrowded concentration camp to another until the war ended and liberation came.

But for Viktor, like many others, life would never be the same—for only he and his sister had survived. The rest of his family perished either from the harsh conditions of the concentration camps, or as a direct result of the gas chambers. This added intense emotional pain that compounded the years of previous trauma. Nevertheless, Viktor not only survived, he was also able to overcome the mental anguish that followed. In spite of these ongoing tragedies, Viktor learned to find peace in the midst of suffering and used his vigorous sense of meaning to propel himself beyond the pain. He is a man who rose above a horrendous set of circumstances and went on to teach others the skills needed to do the same.

The Existential Therapies

After obtaining his freedom, Frankl wrote his well-known book, *Man's Search for Meaning*, where he provides an account of his time in the concentration camps as well as insights into the key concepts of logo therapy — a therapeutic modality developed by Frankl that focuses on meaning as the primary driving force in establishing positive change. Logo therapy is one of a number of existential therapies that encourage its users to leverage their hurts as a catalyst for growth.

Trauma is a life-organizing event that, if untreated, can forever alter the way one perceives the world. For some, harsh experiences produce overpowering feelings of anxiety that lead to a decreased ability to function independently and desperate attempts to self-medicate the pain. However, for others, hardships become a driving force that propels them into positive action. The existential therapies hone in on our God-given abilities to choose our inward responses to our outward circumstances. Frankl wrote, "When we are no longer able to change a situation, we are challenged to change ourselves.[1]" He referred to an individual's ability to choose his or her attitude in any given situation as "the last of the human freedoms."[1] From the existential therapies we learn that a painful past does not necessitate a tainted future and that with enough determination, negative circumstances can become a mechanism for dynamic growth.

History abounds with people who found meaning in the midst of pain and as a result, positively influenced the world around them. These include men and women such as:

- Candy Lightner, a mother whose thirteen-year-old daughter was killed by a drunk driver. Devastated by this tragic event, Candy went on to found Mothers Against Drunk Driving, or MADD for short, an organization that boasts a 50 percent reduction in the rate of drunk driving since its founding.

- John Walsh, a hotel management partner whose six-year-old son Adam was left alone by his mother in the toy section of a department store while she shopped. During the seven minutes he was left unattended, Adam was lured outside and disappeared. Days later it was discovered he had been brutally murdered. The Walsh family responded proactively, testifying before congress about the need for new laws to protect missing and exploited children. They worked tirelessly to pass the Adam Walsh Child Protection Safety Act, a law promoting strict penalties for unregistered sex offenders. But they didn't stop there: John Walsh went on to host *America's Most Wanted*, a television show encouraging its viewers to call in with tips on unsolved crimes that has led to the capture of over a thousand criminals.

- Kay Warren, a pastor's wife whose adult son wrestled with severe depression for years before ultimately taking his own life. As a result of this tragedy, Kay has embarked on a personal mission to educate churches and families on the challenges those with mental illnesses face. Her actions are part of a movement forging a path for decreased stigmatization and increased compassion amongst the Christian community.

Each of these men and women discovered significance in their sufferings that allowed them to progress beyond their pain and led them to positively influence those around them. Suffering is a normal part of the human experience, and everyone will experience some level of anguish during their lifetime. In extreme circumstances, when overwhelming agony abounds, meaning becomes a survival mechanism that allows one to endure in the midst of excruciating difficulties.

Frankl witnessed this firsthand while in the concentration camps. He looked on as seemingly healthy human beings lost hope and, as a direct result, underwent a rapid decline in all areas of functioning. He describes how the eyes of these individuals would become hollow and empty. They would then withdraw from work, stop mingling with friends, and opt to keep isolated on their bunks. Cigarette coupons once stored up and exchanged for food would be carelessly smoked away — with the loss of meaning came the expiration of the will to survive. Sadly, once this happened, it wasn't long before these otherwise healthy individuals would depart from life.

On the other hand, Viktor noted that those in less vigorous physical health who possessed a strong sense of purpose would carry on long after survival seemed reasonable. These highly motivated individuals would care for others around them by sharing what little food they had. Unbeknownst to them, in reaching out to others they were also strengthening themselves. Hope is contagious, and it's almost impossible to serve others without being refreshed ourselves. Through acts of kindness, these brave men and women transformed anguish into triumph, or as Viktor put it, found "healing through meaning."[2]

Finding Strength in Weakness

The existential therapies hone in on the value of discovering significance in life, suffering, and death. It is a modality of paradoxes that demonstrates that it's not only possible for strength to come out of weakness, but that at times, disadvantages can serve as one's greatest asset. This idea has a biblical foundation which is expounded upon in 2 Corinthians 12. In this passage, the Apostle Paul writes about a mysterious ailment causing him much distress. Although the precise nature of the problem is never detailed, theologians speculate that Paul was referring to a gradual decline of his eyesight, and if this was the case, it would certainly have made the writing and traveling duties of an apostle exceedingly difficult. But regardless of the particulars, it is enough to know that this weakness, which Paul referred to as a "thorn in his flesh," disturbed him to the point that he cried out to God on three separate occasions asking for its removal. But when God replied, it was with an unexpected answer. Paul writes,

> *"But he (God) said to me, 'My grace is enough for you, for my power is made perfect in weakness.' So then, I will boast most gladly about my weaknesses, so that the power of Christ may reside in me. Therefore I am content with weaknesses, with insults, with troubles, with persecutions and difficulties for the sake of Christ, for whenever I am weak, then I am strong."*[3]

Pain increased Paul's reliance on God and provided the opportunity for a demonstration of His divine power. By trusting God and moving forward in spite of his limitations, Paul joined the ranks of men and women who draw on their challenges as a means of propelling themselves forward. After this God-encounter, Paul's affliction took on a new significance, reminding him to look to heavenward for strength as opposed to attempting to progress on his own merit. The Apostle Paul is an excellent example of how great challenges can develop into grand assets.

Meaning and Suffering

The danger of a life of ease is that too much comfort can lead to complacence and stagnation. On the other hand, suffering has the ability to steer a person toward searching, discovery, and growth. Although joy and suffering are two words not typically associated with one another, in the Bible Jesus speaks of both—which leads one to wonder if the two are more closely linked than we realize. In John 10:10, Jesus stated that He came so that we could have life and have it more abundantly. Yet, Christ goes on to describe a life far different than what one would expect from an abundant life by boldly proclaiming:

- "In the world you have trouble and suffering" (John 16:33).

- "Do not think that I have come to bring peace to the earth. I have not come to bring peace but a sword For I have come to set a man against his father, a daughter against her mother, and a daughter-in-law against her mother-in-law and a man's enemies will be the members of his household" (Matthew 10:34-36).

- "If the world hates you, be aware that it hated me first... If they persecuted me, they will also persecute you" (John 15:18-20).

These are gut-wrenching words that are neither nice nor pleasant. However, the positive side of these statements is that they invite us to embrace a purpose bigger than ourselves. Jim Elliot, a missionary killed while bringing the message of salvation to the Auca Indians, understood this when he penned the phrase, "He is no fool who gives what he cannot keep to gain what he cannot lose," in his personal journals. Jim's passion reached such intensity that he expressed a willingness to perish for the cause of Christ long before the events leading to his martyrdom transpired.

In 2 Corinthians 4:8-10, the Apostle Paul provides another example of the fusion of suffering and joy when he writes, "We are hard pressed on every side, but not crushed; perplexed, but not in despair; persecuted, but not abandoned; struck down, but not destroyed. We always carry around in our body the death of Jesus, so that the life of Jesus may also be revealed in our body." This passage paints a picture of both suffering and hope, a world where ache and elation exist side by side.

A Life Greater Than Ourselves

As Christ followers, we understand that we exist for a purpose grander than ourselves: a message that has ignited the passion of millions. In 2002, Pastor Rick Warren published *The Purpose Driven Life*, a book that became a record-setting bestseller. What's interesting is that it opens with the declaration, "It's not about you," a bold, in-your-face statement for a self-absorbed culture. Yet, people accepted, pursued, and devoured this teaching.

Another illustration of the need for a grander meaning is found in the correlation between affluence and happiness. Studies show that once a person achieves a level of financial success where they are able to reasonably meet their basic needs, any additional accumulation of wealth adds little to one's overall feelings of wellbeing. The old adage, money can't buy happiness, continues to ring true today. In Matthew 10:39, Jesus said, "Whoever finds their life will lose it, and whoever loses their life for my sake will find it." Deep in the heart of man is a God-given longing for a purpose that extends beyond immediate gratification, and when that meaning is found, true life begins.

Personal Journeys of Meaning

So how does one go about discovering meaning? Twelve-step programs suggest that this journey begins with looking to a higher power, and this is certainly a good place to start. After all, we have already determined that it's necessary for meaning to come from a source greater than oneself. Yet settling on who or what one's higher power will be can be difficult. During my internship in the twelve-step programs, I've had clients inform me that their higher powers were everything from a personal relationship with Jesus Christ, to a relationship with God in general, to something as simple as nature, and the beauty of creation.

I remember one client in particular who spent an extensive amount of time wrestling with the issue. This man recounted having not grown up in a spiritual home, stated that he had no particular religious beliefs, and was having difficulty grasping the concept of God. He reported observing other participants in the program look to their higher power for strength and expressed a great desire to personally experience this. It was as though he was walking by a home filled with family, friends and warmth on a cold winter evening, glimpsing through a window the happiness inside as he passed. Although he was able to observe the excitement of others, he reported being unable to attain it himself.

Eventually, in order to progress through the steps, this man made the decision to embrace his mother as his higher power. As unusual as this may sound, this became the starting point for change as he too experienced the benefits of finding meaning. The good news is that no matter what higher power one finds, the simple act of looking to a power greater than oneself adds significance to life.

Meaning with Power or Meaning with POWER!

Of course, this brings up the question; does it really matter where one attains meaning, or will looking to any higher power do? Personally, I'm a firm believer that something is almost always better than nothing, and that in this man's case, looking to his mother for significance was a good start. However, it was only one small step forward in acquiring the wealth of importance readily available to all who will receive it.

When it comes to meaning, there is meaning with power, and meaning with POWER! As we will see, all meaning has some level of usefulness, but there are certain types of meaning that are far more advantageous than others. One area where this is clearly seen is with the placebo effect. The placebo effect occurs during medication studies and happens when study participants unintentionally report trial medications as being more helpful than they really are. In order to compensate for this effect and achieve accurate results, modern-day study participants are divided into a test group and a control group. Test group participants are administered the actual medication, while the control group receives a sugar pill, also known as a placebo. Although it has no medicinal value, the placebo is given because the act of taking a pill and believing that pill will help you get better has been shown to cause patients to feel better. The impact of one's belief is so great that researchers must utilize both of these groups to accurately determine a medication's level of effectiveness.

There can be no doubt: putting one's faith in a placebo, whether it be a sugar pill, or any higher power at all, produces some level of positive results. A higher power does not need to be real nor powerful in order to provide benefit. Nevertheless, no one goes to the doctor seeking a placebo; the effective medication is always desired. Similarly, although faith alone has some advantage, to be truly powerful, our faith must be placed in a God who is real, mighty, and able to sustain us in times of need.

Let me explain with a story that took place when I was in high school. I attended a fairly large youth group, and one Sunday morning when everyone was standing for worship, I noticed a mischievous teen secretly steal away the chair from behind a boy in front of him. The young man who had his chair removed had no idea what had happened. When the worship ended, the youth pastor directed everyone to their seats and everybody sat down, including the youth who had his chair snuck away. In spite of the fact that this young man had faith that his chair would hold him up, he came crashing to the floor. His faith wasn't enough to hold him up; he needed a chair that was steady, solid, and behind him when he sat down. Fortunately, no one was hurt, and the boy who had the practical joke played on him recovered nicely. Similarly, in looking to a higher power, faith alone is not sufficient. While it's true that looking to any higher power can make us feel better, only a God who is real, powerful, and on our side is able to sustain us in times of need.

Encountering the God Who Is

God spoke with Moses in the wilderness, through a bush that was engulfed in flame but not consumed. During this encounter, God commanded Moses to return to Egypt and speak as His voice. Although God assured Moses that He would provide the words to say, Moses trembled and was filled with doubt. At one point Moses asked, "If I go to the Israelites and tell them, 'The God of your fathers has sent me to you,' and they ask me, 'What is his name?'– what should I say to them?" To which God replied, "I AM that I AM... You must say this to the Israelites, 'I AM has sent me to you.'"[4]

When asked His name, God responded, "I AM." What an incredible name for our Creator! God is not simply a higher power, idea, or concept... He is. James 2:17 says that faith without works is dead, and faith in any being who is not alive, active and willing to act on our behalf is dead too. During the storms of life, you and I need I AM, the God who is real, willing, and able to come to our aid.

Living a Life of Meaning

As we have seen, meaning is important because it increases our ability to function well, propels us forward, and provides strength in times of duress. Now let's look at three specific ways that following Christ contributes to meaning.

249

1. In Christ we find meaning in life itself.

As a father of three girls, I know what it's like to delight in one's children. I wish I could find a better way to describe it, but other words just don't seem to work. Although "pleased" and "happy" are good descriptions of how I feel about my kids most of the time, they are not always true. There are occasions when the girls argue, become stubborn, or don't listen, and during these moments I am neither happy nor pleased with the choices they are making. Yet this never changes the fact that I am delighted that they are my children. No matter what my kids do, I wouldn't trade the honor of being their dad for anything.

I remember the day my oldest daughter was born. In an instant my entire outlook changed. During the weeks that followed, my friends would ask the usual questions of how my week was and what I did. While past conversations centered on mountain biking, hiking, skydiving and other adventures, once Mackenzie was born, my responses altered dramatically. A huge grin would come across my face as I would recount how my daughter smiled, rolled over, or laughed for the first time. Although my friends did their best to share in my excitement, I could tell they just didn't get it—and that was okay. A few years earlier I wouldn't have understood either. After knowing the joy of having children, my perspective on what really matters has never been the same. My girls don't have to do anything for me to delight in them. Just seeing them brings a smile to my face, and if you have children, it's likely that you can relate.

I share this story because this is precisely how God feels about us. According to 1 John 3:1, we are His children. Psalm 147:11 proclaims that "The Lord takes pleasure in those who fear Him," and in Psalm 139:17 David writes, "How difficult it is for me to fathom your thoughts about me, O God! How vast is their sum total! If I tried to count them, they would outnumber the grains of sand." As Christ followers we are well aware that God loves us, but sometimes I think we forget that He also likes us, and that we bring a smile to His face. God delights in the fact that we are His children, and because of this, there is meaning in life itself.

2. In Christ there is meaning in following His commands.

A second area in which Christ followers attain meaning is in fulfilling Christ's commands. Micah 6:8 says, "He has told you, O man, what is good, and what the Lord really wants from you: He wants you to promote justice, to be faithful, and to live obediently before your God." Throughout the Bible we see that God requires His people to do and not do certain things. Although God loves you and I just the way we are, He also doesn't want us to remain stagnant, but longs for us to grow to become more like Jesus. Time and time again, Jesus spoke the words "follow me," and following Christ by living out His will on a daily basis is a second area in which Christ followers find meaning. Some of the ways this is accomplished is through:

- Loving God and others (Matthew 22:37-39)
- Praying (1 Thessalonians 5:17)
- Meeting together with fellow Christ followers (Hebrews 10:25)
- Teaching others to follow God (Matthew 28:19), and
- Giving to those in need (2 Corinthians 9:7)

Yet, this is only the beginning. 2 Peter 3:18 says that we are to grow in the grace and knowledge of Jesus. There is always more to be learned which means that honoring God is an ongoing process and not a onetime event. Through consistent acts of prayer, Bible study, worship, and fellowship we fulfill Christ's commands, grow in our relationship with Him, and add meaning to our lives.

3. Following Christ brings meaning to suffering.

As we have seen, the existential theories encourage us to find meaning in life, suffering, and death; and through Christ, we attain meaning in each of these areas. In

Philippians 4:11-13, the Apostle Paul states, "I am not saying this because I am in need, for I have learned to be content in any circumstance. I have experienced times of need and times of abundance. In any and every circumstance I have learned the secret of contentment, whether I go satisfied or hungry, have plenty or nothing. I am able to do all things through the one who strengthens me."

Paul's secret of being content in each and every situation came in looking to Christ for strength. Paul knew that he and God could get through anything together, including trials, times of suffering, and even death itself. In fact, Paul was so confident of this that he wrote, "For to me, living is Christ and dying is gain."[5] Paul is an incredible example of a man who lived out existential principles and in so doing, discovered meaning in life, suffering, and death—and you and I can have this incredible sense of significance too. For, Christ invites us into a life of extraordinary purpose where no slice of existence is without meaning.

Life's Great Lesson from Existential Theory

People need a purpose bigger than themselves. Through Christ we find meaning in living, following Christ daily, suffering and death.

Questions for Additional Reflection and Discussion

1. Think of someone you know who has discovered a deep meaning in life. In what ways has possessing purpose positively impacted their life?

2. Can you think of times in your life when faith was helpful? In what ways is faith a good thing?

3. Can you think of times in your life when faith was placed in someone or something unreliable? What were the results? Can you think of other situations where faith could be misguided or harmful?

4. How do we test our faith to make sure that it is helpful and not a hindrance to ourselves and to others?

5. What specific examples do you have of times where finding meaning and purpose in life, suffering, and death was helpful?

6. Is there a specific situation you are going through right now where you could look to Christ to find additional meaning? What would it look like specifically to trust Christ in this particular situation?

Nine

Lifelong Learning

Ongoing Lessons from the Bible and Psychology

If you make Insight your priority,
and won't take no for an answer,
Searching for it like a prospector panning for gold,
like an adventurer on a treasure hunt,
Believe me, before you know it Fear-of-GOD will be
yours.

~ Proverbs 2:3-5 *The Message*

Life has a natural progression of joy and sorrow. The key is to trust the process, continue pressing forward, and to never stop growing.

This book began with a story of my personal journey of discovery. I recounted how my own crises led me to seeking counsel that either encouraged increased acts of spiritual discipline or promoted efforts to be kinder, nicer, gentler, and a better servant as the solution. I told how following this limited guidance led me down a path of unnecessary confusion as I honed in on actions that didn't directly relate to the challenges I faced. Eventually my path led me to the principles shared in this book and, over time, applying these ideas led to healing and growth.

Yet positive changes didn't come all at once, nor did moving forward happen in a straight line. Often it was a trudging process of taking a few steps forward before stumbling a step or two back. There were moments when the path was hazy and where advancement was a perplexing process of trial and error. But over time and with consistent application of these principles, things did get better. It's now been over eight years since the opening challenges I wrote about, and I am pleased to say that life is good — not perfect, by any means — but good. These initial difficulties have long passed, and of course, in the years that followed, new trials have arisen in their place — but that is all a normal part of the human experience.

No amount of wisdom will eliminate troubles completely, and this is by no means an overly optimistic self-help book that touts, "If you follow these four quick and easy steps, then your life will be perfect just like mine." Although optimism is good, so is remaining realistic. Those who embrace both, understand that at times, life is fun, funny, and beautiful, and in other seasons it's hard. During the good times, it is important to be aware that troubles lurk in the future (so as to not be naively caught off-guard), and during challenging times we can remain confident that one day the pain will pass. Since there is a normal progression of happiness and suffering, the goal is not a life of ease, but instead, to enjoy the pleasant moments to their fullest and to move through difficulties with dignity and grace.

It's important to keep in mind that neither joy nor sorrow serve as an accurate measurement of faith. I emphasize this because painful moments are easier if we don't heap additional loads of guilt and shame upon ourselves. Trials often hit when we least expect them, and although they are always painful, they are not always bad.

Ecclesiastes 3 says, "For everything there is an appointed time, and an appropriate time for every activity on earth:" The chapter goes on to describe fourteen events commonly viewed as positive and fourteen opposite events usually perceived as negative. However, before concluding, the author states, "God has made everything fit beautifully in its appropriate time." According to Scripture everything has a purpose. Beauty results from pain and joy comes out of troubles. This is such a common occurrence that James 1:2-4 says, "Consider it nothing but joy when you fall into all sorts of trials, because you know that the testing of your faith produces endurance. And let endurance have its perfect effect, so that you will be perfect and complete, not deficient in anything." Though unpleasant, difficulties have their benefits. It is during the hard times that we:

- Learn to rely on God for strength moment by moment
- Form deep and lasting friendships
- Seek out wisdom
- Discover new ways of thinking and acting, which lead to the development of better habits
- Increase our compassion for others who are hurting

- Gain greater insights into coping strategies and valuable life skills
- Develop our skills as a leader, and
- Grow in our understanding of how we best function

Looking back, I can now see the many positive results that came out of the pain that occurred in my life. The difficulties I faced led me to return to college, become a licensed marriage and family therapist, and start a new career that I love. These challenges opened the door for me to teach at the seminary, and it's because of them that I sat down to write this book. It was also during the storms of life that I met my wife. Today I understand that these hardships worked together to lead to the incredible life that we now share together.

Isaiah 61:3 talks about how God gives beauty for ashes. I have found this to be true in my life and believe this is true for you as well. I share this because no matter what obstacles you face, I want you to know that there is hope. The pain may not pass quickly, but it will decrease over time and eventually vanish, leaving joy and beauty in its place. We can be certain of this because God promises that one day, He will wipe every tear away.[1] Until then, the key is to trust the process, keep pressing forward, and continue learning, developing, and growing. My hope is that this book has played an important part in this process and that instead of viewing this chapter as a conclusion, you will see it as the beginning of a lifelong journey of discovery and growth. As you continue down the path of studying psychology and theology, here are four important principles to keep in mind:

1. Embrace core values, and approach quick fixes with caution.

In November 2006, Rhonda Byrne published her well-known book *The Secret,* which quickly rose to the top of the best-sellers list. The book promised that anyone could attain health, happiness, and success by learning to apply the world's best-kept secret. So, what was this hidden treasure that guaranteed such magnificent results? The simplified version of the secret is that the universe is at our service and if one simply sends out the right vibes by intensely focusing on what he or she wants, those desires will come to fruition. The book goes so far as to depict the universe as a waiter at a restaurant eagerly waiting to take our order.

What's interesting is that *The Secret's* so-called secret was not hidden after at all. The key idea of intensely focusing on one's goals is a well-known concept from psychology repackaged in such a way that it overpromised and under-delivered. The book created such high expectations in readers that anyone who took its message at face value was bound to be disappointed.

Years have passed since this book was first published, and although people were receptive to its message, this did not result in an influx of highly successful, happy, and healthy individuals. In spite of the hundreds of thousands of people who sent their positive vibes into the world, the United States economy still took a massive nose dive before entering its slow recovery. Those who "put in their order to the universe" struggled side by side with those who did not, showing that this book was simply the latest and greatest in a long list of oversimplified ideas promising quick and easy results.

The Apostle Paul spoke of ideas like these in Colossians 2:8, stating, "Be careful not to allow anyone to captivate you through an empty, deceitful philosophy that is according to human traditions and the elemental spirits of the world, and not according to Christ." I wouldn't be at all surprised to learn that Paul wrote these words in response to a similar set of "secrets" going around in his day. While often these ideas are not entirely bad, they don't accomplish what they promise and become a setup for disappointment.

In fact, those who adhered to the ideas in *The Secret* likely discovered two things. First, they would have found that by focusing on their goals daily, they did make some progress. After all, many of the key ideas are based on sound psychological principles. Second, if the goal was big enough, they would have also seen that progress doesn't come easy. Change is hard, and there are no formulas leading to a quick fix. On the other hand, there are principles that can be used to assure that change is not more complex than it needs to be—and yes, there is a big difference between the two.

The Secret has been brought up by clients during our therapy sessions on a number of occasions, and when this happens I like to use humor to point out the fallacy of looking for effortless results. I share how I've discovered that the universe cannot keep up with me. In spite of the fact that I've been putting out vibes for a winning lottery ticket for years, "the waiter" has yet to deliver my request. True success is built over time and results from the consistent practice of core values. Any book, seminar, or tool that promises dramatic, instantaneous results, will end in disappointment. Nevertheless, by learning from the sound advice of others and developing our character daily, we will achieve progress over time.

2. Keep Learning and Growing.

My passion for psychology began in 1994. I was a sophomore in high school, and my mom gave me a copy of Dale Carnagie's classic, *How to Win Friends and Influence People.* Since then, I've read through this book at least a dozen times. My original copy — with a torn-off cover, highlighted, tattered, and filled with dog-eared pages from frequent use — continues to sit on my bookshelf to this day. Since high school, I've read hundreds of other books on psychology, theology, and personal growth. My bookshelves are now stacked two and three books deep as I continue to seek out new insights.

As I study, I occasionally come across a book that claims to be the final word on a particular subject. These books make bold statements like, "This will be the last book on leadership/ time management/ relationships/ ect. that you will ever need." Years ago I would get excited when I saw introductions like these. I was naive enough to believe that this meant the book was filled with truly incredible information. Today when I read a statement like this, I think to myself, *If this writer believes that he or she is going to teach me everything I need to know in 200 pages or less, he or she must not know very much about this subject.* I have yet to read a book that has left me feeling that I've arrived at a place where there is nothing left to learn, and the truth is that you and I are not at this place yet, and will not arrive there — at least not until Christ returns. As previously stated, Philippians 1:6 declares that Christ will continue his good work in us until the glorious day when Christ Jesus returns. But until this takes place, it's our job to be persistent in our learning and growth.

We live in an ever-changing world, and growing adds joy to life. We won't be the same tomorrow and neither will those around us. Some of our relationships will mature, while others will change, and a few will fade away. As we become older our children will become less dependent on us as parents, and conversely, us parents will age and, in due course, begin to increasingly look to our adult children for support. Changes are a natural progression of life and as they occur, continued growth is needed. Learning to live, love, and lead well truly is a lifelong process.

3. Draw from as Many Different Sources as Possible.

Today, a large number of modern-day therapists are adopting an eclectic approach in their practices. In past decades, therapists would adopt one primary therapeutic modality, which meant that if a person went to see a client-centered therapist, he or she would benefit only from the teachings of that one modality. There was little overlap, and therapists prided themselves in closely adhering to their chosen model. Today we have a better understanding of just how complex people are. We recognize that there is more than one path leading to positive change, and know that what works well for one individual may not be as effective for the next.

Wise advice is a lot like a tool in a toolbox. The more wisdom one acquires, the more tools for overcoming challenges a person has at his or her disposal. Proverbs 15:22 says, "Plans fail when there is no counsel, but with abundant advisers they are established." The more open we are to learning, the more wisdom we will find.

The need to remain open to wisdom is something I discovered during the three years I spent working for a Wraparound program. Wraparound is a family support system that takes a team-based approach to problem-solving. It connects families to professionals with extensive clinical experiences as well as to partners who have less formal training but years of valuable life experience. In Wraparound, I quickly learned that formal training is not enough. In many instances our youth and family partners were able to provide helpful insights from their unique perspective that I did not possess. I discovered that there is much to be learned from those with experiences different from my own, and picked up valuable skills from our partners that I was not taught in the college classroom. Wisdom can be found all around us when we remain open to it.

4. Keep Testing Everything

Proverbs 18:17 says, "The first to state his case seems right, until his opponent begins to cross-examine him." Time and time again we see that Christ's followers are called to an intelligent faith. Like a scientist conducting experiments in a lab, believers are called to test everything, use the sound minds that God has given them, cautiously weigh out both sides of the issues, and seek out wisdom for the sake of honoring Christ.

But doing this is hard work. It's much easier to say things like, "When the Bible and science conflict, I believe the Bible every time." While words like this may sound spiritual, they show a naive understanding of Scripture. As Christians, we would be wise to keep in mind that science and the Bible can never conflict. In John 17:17 Jesus said, "Your word is truth," and as we have seen, science is a means of seeking truth through the use of the scientific process. Any perceived discrepancy between science and the Bible indicates that a full understanding of truth has not yet been gained and means that additional work needs to be done. The error may be in our understanding of Scripture, or be the result of a flaw in the scientific experiment. Either way, the result of good hermeneutics and good science will result in an agreement of truth every time. 1 Corinthians 13:12 says, "For now we see in a mirror indirectly, but then we will see face to face. Now I know in part, but then I will know fully, just as I have been fully known." One day, you and I will "get it" and understand how God and science have been in agreement all along. Until then, it is our job to use discernment and continue to test everything.

I've read that those who specialize in detecting fraud learn to identify counterfeit bills by spending hours studying real money. They spend so much time focusing on genuine currency that a fake is easily spotted. It's the same with us: when we focus on what is true, we will become so equipped in recognizing the authentic that we will be able to easily identify and discard errors. Whether we are seeking out truth or wise advice for living, a continual process of testing everything is needed.

As you can see, psychology and the Bible really do go hand in hand. They team up to provide us with sound advice for caring for ourselves so that we can reach out to others from a place of abundance. They teach us how to support others in ways that are truly healing, and provide us with sound advice for gently guiding others toward positive change. As we have seen, life can be difficult at times, as well as exciting and beautiful at others. The good news is that with wisdom, we can move gracefully through life's challenges and make the most out of each and every joyful moment that comes our way. May God continue to bless you as you grow in the grace and knowledge of Him and continue your journey of learning to live, love, and lead well!

Questions for Additional Reflection and Discussion

1. Have you ever attempted to follow advice from a book, magazine, lecture or teacher that promised to provide a secret to quickly fix a complex problem? If so, what was the end result of following this advice?

2. In what ways do you see integrating positive character qualities into our lives as being more valuable than looking to promises of a quick fix?

3. What are some specific steps you are currently taking to continue your own growth?

4. This chapter suggested drawing from multiple sources in order to get the most out of ongoing personal growth. What are some of the different sources of wisdom from which you are gleaning?

5. Have you found yourself putting off the study of Christianity or psychology in the past due to overly focusing on some of the weird or ugly parts associated with them? If so, how could you adjust your study methods in order to not to discard the good with the bad?

6. How will you integrate the principle of testing everything, holding on to the good and getting rid of the bad into your everyday studies? Is there a specific

subject you are studying or an area of life where this tool is especially applicable right now?

Acknowledgements

A little over a year ago I set out to write a book. As a new author, I had no idea what this would entail. I simply knew that I had an important message to share. So with a borrowed laptop, no budget, and little idea of the adventure ahead, I began to write. The fact that you are now holding this book in your hands is a huge tribute to two things. First, it is a demonstration of the power of the principles found in this book. On a daily basis, I found myself using the principles found in this book, such as monitoring my own self-talk and forcing myself to make some progress daily, especially during the times the words didn't flow easily.

Second, this book is a huge tribute to an incredible support system. Friends and family quickly jumped on board, supporting this project through a crowd funding campaign that provided funding for editing and design. Some gave generously of their own time to help proof and refine my initial writing, and others cheered me on along the way. I'd like to say an especially big thank you to the following friends, family, and new acquaintances whose encouragement and support has meant more than you know. Thank you,

Steven & Carol Jurchenko, David & Jane Mork, Jacey Coy, Stephen Babby, Jean Penning, Carolyn Bellanti, Debra L Frese, Jose Villalobos, Salil Jha, Todd Mathisen, Randall Hutchinson, Michael K. Martin, Jin Sook Park, and the numerous anonymous donors who gave generously to make this book possible!

It's because of your generous support that I was able to get this book published!

In addition, I'd like to thank Ken Ilgunas for allowing me to include part of his story in this book. I also want to say a huge thank you to Dr. Barry Lord for taking time out of his own publishing and speaking schedule to write the foreword.

Thank you to the students who attend the Theological Foundations of Counseling class at Southern California Seminary. Your excellent questions challenge my thinking and keep me pressing forward on my own journey of learning and growth

Finally, I'm incredibly grateful for my incredible wife Jennifer, and three amazing daughters; Mackenzie, Brooklyn, and Addison. Thank you for allowing me to sneak away and write this book. You have been my biggest cheerleaders in this process and God has truly blessed me with an amazing family!

Continue the Conversation

I hope you enjoyed this book and would love to hear from you. You can continue the conversation on:

- My blog: www.coffeeshopconversations.com
- E-mail: jed@coffeeshopconversations.com
- Twitter: @jjurchenko

Before you go, I'd like to say a huge "thank you" for reading this book all the way to the end. I'd greatly appreciate it if you would take a minute to leave a review on Amazon. Your feedback helps me to create high-quality resources and to spread the word about how psychology and the Bible work together to create dynamic life change. So, if you loved this book, please let me know!

Continue the Journey

Would you like to take your understanding of theology and psychology to the next level? If so, Southern California Seminary can help. With face-to-face and on-line options, solid biblical teachings, and an affordable tuition, Southern California Seminary is an exceptional resource for everyone longing for a high-quality education built upon the foundation of God's word!

You can find out more by visiting www.socalsem.edu or by calling (619) 201-8959. We look forward to hearing from you soon.

End Notes

Chapter 1

1. Butcher, Mineka, and Hooley, *Abnormal Psychology*, 14th Edition, Allyn & Bacon
2. www.dictionary.com
3. Acts 17:11
4. John 14:6
5. Luke 10:27-28
6. 1 John 4:8
7. 1 John 3:16

Chapter 2

1. I don't remember the name of the teacher or class this quote came from. I do know it made an impact on me as I remember it over 10 years later.
2. This quote was memorized as part of Dr. George Goolde's undergraduate Hermeneutics class.
3. Packer, J.I. *Desiring God*, Inter Varsity Press, 1973. Pg 19.

4. Diagnostic and Statistical Manual of Mental Disorders, Fourth Edition, Text Revision. Washing, DC, American Psychiatric Association, 2000 pg 725.
5. This is my paraphrase of a cartoon I saw on Facebook. However, I have been unable to track down original, get the exact quote, and as a result, am unable to provide credit to the original author.
6. Chamine Shirzad, *Positive Intelligence,* Greenleaf Book Group LLC 2012.
7. New American Standard Bible
8. NET Bible
9. The KJV New Testament Greek Lexicon

Chapter 3

1. I remember our youth pastor telling these stories on a number of occasions. I think they may have originally come from Bill Hybles book *Who You are When No One Is Looking,* a book our youth group was studying at the time.
2. Ellis Albert and Harper Robert, *A Guide To Rational Living,* Melvin Powers Wilshire Book Company, 1997. pg 57.

Chapter 4

1. Glasser William, *Choice Theory A New Psychology of Personal Freedom,* HarperPerennial Publishers 1999. Pg 14.

2. Glasser William, *Warning: Psychiatry Can Be Hazardous To Your Mental Health*, HarperCollins Publishers 2003. Pg 7.
3. The exact conversion is unknown. Most estimates placed the modern day worth of a Biblical talent of silver between $370,000 and $480,000 U.S. dollars.
4. Ilgunas Ken, *Walden on Wheels: The Open Road from Debt to Freedom*, New Harvest Publishers 2013. Permission to include Ken's story was granted by Ken Ilgunas on 7/20/2014, "Hi Jed. Sure, go for it! I'd be honored."
5. Joshua 24:15

Chapter 5

1. Bowlby John, *A Secure Base*, Basic Books 1988, pg 62.
2. Genesis 3:12
3. Luke 10:40-42
4. John 11:35
5. Matthew 9:9
6. Matthew 16:23
7. Mark 11:15-19
8. John 2:1-11
9. Luke 22:42
10. Genesis 2:18
11. Miner, Maureen. "The Impact of Child-Parent Attachment, Attachment to God and Religious Orientation on Psychological Adjustment." *Journal of Psychology and Theology* 37.2 (2009): 114-24. *ProQuest*. Web. 15 Dec. 2013.

Chapter 6

1. Ecclesiastes 3:7
2. Haggbloom, S.J. et al. (2002). The 100 Most Eminent Psychologists of the 20th Century. *Review of General Psychology*. Vol. 6, No. 2, 139–152.
3. Job 2:13
4. Mehrabian & Wiener, 1967 and Mehrabian & Ferris, 1967 are two research studies that combined to form the 55/38/7 formula.
5. Matthew 8:3

Chapter 7

1. Acts 17:11
2. Romans 7:15
3. Dr. Barry Lord – A common "Berryism" spoken in the classes he taught.
4. A special thanks to Dr. Barry Lord from whom I first heard the beach-ball and gun-powder illustrations.
5. Matthew 23:27
6. Genesis 3:6
7. Genesis 3:12
8. John 14:6

Chapter 8

1. Frankel, Victor E., *Man's Search for Meaning,* Beacon Press 1946.
2. Fabry Joseph, *The Pursuit of Meaning: Logotherapy Applied to Life.* Beacon Press, 1968.
3. 2 Corinthians 12:9-10

4. Exodus 3:13-14
5. Philippians 1:21

Chapter 9

1. Revelation 21:4

About the Author

Jed Jurchenko supports passionate but discouraged Christ followers in living, leading, and relating well by helping them apply life-changing truths from the Bible and psychology to their everyday challenges. Jed is a licensed Marriage and Family Therapist and college professor with over twenty years of experience in working with children, teens, and families in a variety of settings. Jed graduated from Southern California Seminary with a Masters of Divinity and returned to complete a second master's degree in the area of counseling and psychology. Jed is especially passionate about helping others see the connection between psychology, the Bible, and everyday life.

But most of all, Jed is a husband, and father to three amazing girls. In his free time he enjoys hiking, reading, barbequing, and spending time at the beach with his family.

Made in the USA
Las Vegas, NV
18 November 2023

81085512R00157